Presented to:
Butler Area Public Library

**In Memory of
Sandy, A Faithful Soul**

**Donor
Butler Dog Training Association**

Therapy Dogs Today

Their Gifts, Our Obligation

Therapy Dogs Today

Their Gifts, Our Obligation

Kris Butler

Funpuddle Publishing Associates

Published by
Funpuddle Publishing Associates
12201 Buckskin Pass
Norman, OK 73026

Visit our web site at www.DogPrograms.com

Library of Congress Control Number 2004091027

Cataloging–in–Publication Data

Butler, Kris
    Therapy dogs today : their gifts our obligation / Kris Butler
        88 p. 22 cm.
    Summary: Explores value of therapy dogs in physical therapy, occupational therapy, speech therapy, recreational therapy, mental health, and special education, and discusses the process of training dogs, handlers, and animal–assisted therapy program administrators.
    ISBN 0–9747793–0–X
    1. Animals—Therapeutic use. 2. Working animals. 3. Animals—Training. 4. Dogs.
    HV1569.6.K46 2004
    636.088'6—dc21   2004091027

Printed in the United States of America

Cover and book design by Dustin Tate
Cover photo by Kris Butler
Editor, Lynette Lobbin

Dedicated to Partner

"Sure we can."

Table of Contents

Foreword

This past summer, Little Sir Echo passed away at 18-and-a-half years old. Echo, an American Eskimo Dog, was my first therapy dog, most wonderful friend, and incredible teacher. I "rescued" him from a pet store, sure that his glistening white, fluffy coat, charming grin, and black shoe-button nose and eyes would be a hit in any visiting pet program. The year was 1986 and I was about to begin my career as a social worker incorporating animals in mental health programs. I trained Echo according to the well-thought-out practices of the day. He was adept at all obedience commands including jumps, long stays and downs, and perfect heeling. He knew all the advanced therapy dog commands such as "go see," "head down," and "snuggle." His eyes never left my face. For over two years, Echo and I visited children in homeless shelters, provided counseling to survivors of sexual assault, and visited nursing homes. People loved Echo's exquisite manners, his cheerful doggie grin, and his soft, warm coat. And besides, I loved him.

And then one day training, screening, and my love for Echo were not enough. Echo was sitting on the desk following our presentation to second graders about pet first aid. I had invited the class up to pet Echo and the students surrounded the desk, 40 small hands reaching to pet the little dog. I was talking to a teacher and not paying attention to the children or Echo when a small boy interrupted the conversation and told me Echo had growled at him. I was horrified and at the same time confidant the child was mistaken. "Oh, I'm sure he didn't," I assured the child. Echo sat quietly on the table looking carefully into my face. "I'm sure it was the sound of a chair moving or something like that," I pronounced. The child gave me a doubtful look and shrugged. On the way home I watched Echo. He stood in the passenger seat gazing out the window as we sped toward home. His curled-over tail waved gently as I spoke to him. Had he growled at the boy? Did the boy hurt him? Did

i

another child scare him? I vowed to keep my eyes on him at the next visit.

Several weeks later, another child reported that Echo growled at him during the petting phase of our presentation. I was watching Echo carefully to be sure no one hurt him and I never saw anything that should have made him react in that manner. This time, however, Echo was standing on the floor and the children gathered around him in a tight knot. I picked Echo up and held him for the children to pet. I decided Echo was worried about crowds. Perhaps someone had hurt him in the past in a crowded situation. The next morning, I was standing outside visiting with a neighbor as Echo and her children ran around the backyard. At one point, Echo ran behind me and stood stiffly. One of the children reached his hand toward Echo and then it happened...like a thunderbolt, Echo roared and lunged for the child, his teeth snapping sharply together just short of the child's outstretched fingers.

The relationship between the therapy dog and handler is crucial to the interaction that occurs with the person they visit. All the screening and training in the world will not prepare a dog for the challenges of intimacy and emotion encountered in visiting animal programs. This component of therapy dog work goes beyond routine dog-human communication and cooperation. Working with therapy dogs is not about training, it is about building and maintaining a relationship with another species. By focusing on the concrete details of training, I neglected the more crucial responsibilities of protecting Echo's personal boundaries and feelings of safety.

As Vice President of Delta Society, I met and worked with countless therapy dogs and their handlers. It was my delight each year to work with the Pet Partners® Therapy Dog award winners. Award recipients demonstrated a unique relationship that allowed and supported an entirely new level of intimacy between the handler, participant and the dog. Kris Butler and her dog, Partner, demonstrated this special relationship. Their relationship was built primarily on the long term process of "being." Partner and Kris grew together as a team through the experience of time. Over the months and years they spent together, they learned from each other, and they listened to each other.

Kris and Partner's relationship continued to evolve and change. Kris never assumed the quality of Partner's experience. She never assumed she knew what he wanted or felt in any situation. So many handlers fall into the trap of assuming: assuming the dog enjoys the work, assuming the client likes dogs, assuming they know all they need to know about handling the dog. I assumed that Echo was delighted in working with children because he was always enthusiastic when we went to a school. In hindsight, he indicated in numerous subtle and gentle ways that he was uncomfortable and overwhelmed. I failed to see the changes, I minimized him, I was not open to a different point of view. Not until he demonstrated a dog-type meltdown did I listen to his differing perception.

Effective handlers are capable of sublimating their own egos during the visiting session. In traditional relationships with working dogs such as livestock work, search and rescue, or obedience trials, handlers are congratulated for their skill and expertise. Handlers of therapy dogs must be able to sublimate themselves to the developing intimacy between the participant and the dog. Those handlers who understand that the accolades belong to the person struggling to heal and not to their dog or themselves have reached a significant level of maturity and expertise in this work. Without this understanding, the handler remains in competition with the dog and the patient for reward and recognition.

The work of a therapy dog is an intimate journey between the dog and the person they visit. Handlers must be prepared to witness such intimacy, give time for the expression of pain, support feelings of loss, and demonstrate courage in the face of rage and despair. In rooms where an addict battles withdrawal, a child struggles to walk, or a victim of sexual assault recalls past horrors, there is no place for the handler to ask if the person likes their dog. To work with a therapy dog is to assist people in the slow and personal task of healing.

Working with therapy dogs takes us into unknown spaces. If we have the courage to go beyond what we think dogs are, we may learn new ways of being with this other species that shares its life with us. In the long run, Echo showed me the dangers and limitations inherent in assuming I completely understood another. Because I thought that I had learned enough when I met expected criteria, I missed opportunities to learn from him. Kris recognized Partner for what he was – a dog. For Kris, the unique and expanding relationship with Partner was remarkable enough. Working with therapy dogs is an ongoing process of self-assessment, reflection and willingness to see another species as sometimes more capable and more compassionate than ourselves. It is my hope that all handlers will be open to the potential for their own growth and learning. For by being open to the gifts of animals, we increase our own opportunities for growth and healing.

MAUREEN FREDRICKSON, MSW
Executive Director
MnLYNC

Chapter 1
First Things First

Scout walked so slowly down the hallway of the rehabilitation hospital, he barely moved. Flanked by me on one side and a ten-year-old patient holding a second leash on the other, my chocolate Labrador retriever gave the impression of someone who had all the time in the world. The child by his side was propped upright as she walked, supported by a heroic pediatric physical therapist, who also moved the little girl's legs from behind. At the end of the hall, several other therapists applauded, offering encouragement and cheering their patient on.

This was the first time in the weeks since the automobile accident that the child had been willing to attempt to walk. Since her head injury, she was unable to balance herself and had been afraid to stand or walk, fiercely resisting her therapists' attempts to get her to do so. With no balance compensatory skill, the little girl lived in fear of falling.

The walk ended, not when the patient asked to stop, but when the therapist could no longer continue physically holding the child up, supporting her and moving uncooperative legs. Our short walk down the hall was a huge success.

Scout turned out to be the perfect dog for this job. He was trained to walk at my side at any speed. When we positioned him next to patients who held the leash attached to his second collar or harness, the patients perceived that they were the ones "walking" the dog.

Scout had been taught that eye contact with people was rewarding (training included pats and high praise for that behavior) so that patients sensed a connection with him each time he gazed into their eyes. He also sat automatically during stops, so when patients and therapists rested along the way, Scout's sitting and gazing behaviors were perceived as a strong connection and encouragement. Scout was able to be comfortable and stay focused, even when a number of people moved about in his immediate personal territory.

The walk was actually Scout's second session with the child. During their first meeting, the therapists and I observed the child's enthusiasm for the dog and her willingness to work with him on the floor. We used the first session to plan the second. Prior to the second session, I set the scene with a brightly patterned collar and leash on the mat where the patient and Scout would interact. The seemingly mundane task of putting the collar and leash on Scout encouraged the child to work on fine motor skills and problem solving skills, and provided her with a sense of success. After several minutes, the collar was on the dog and the leash was attached.

When "Wow, Scout's all dressed up. I'll bet he'd love to go for a walk" was followed by an encouraging silence, we knew our patient was not actively resisting the idea.

"If we help you and go with you, will you take Scout for a walk?"

Careful preparation provided a huge payoff. Our patient smiled and nodded her head. "Yes."

Yes!

In hospitals and treatment centers, just like this one, all across the nation, something really important is happening. We are successfully connecting people with visiting dogs in ways that enhance human healing, learning, and self-awareness. Connecting dogs with people is the easy part. There are many people in special care settings and many visiting dogs. Success is trickier.

Success is dependent upon careful preparation connecting with discernible opportunities.

There are always steps to be taken before getting to the task at hand. In order to operate this literary vehicle through the maze of issues and opportunities associated with animal-enhanced programs, we must first identify the people most likely to benefit from this book and offer them a glossary with which to navigate.

This book is important for anyone who is involved, or wants to be involved, in therapeutic or educational programs that include one or more visiting dogs. A visit requires a dog, a handler, and a staff person from the facility being visited. Prior to their first visit, the dog and handler probably will have worked with a trainer or instructor.

A visiting dog must be on a veterinary prescribed immunization and parasite control program. While affiliations with locally formed groups and/or national registry organizations are not essential, they are prevalent, and evaluators, instructors, and group administrators are key people associated with organized groups and registries.

Dogs
Visiting dogs can be any breed or any combination of breeds, any size, and any age. National registries require that dogs be at least one year old to be eligible for registration. (Since dogs make up half of each visiting team, I like to refer to them using the pronoun "who," rather than the impersonal, but grammatically correct, "that.")

Handlers
Throughout this book, handler refers to the person who accompanies, and is in charge of, the dog during visits. Handlers can be either volunteers who visit with their pets; health care professionals and educators who work with their

own dogs in their professional environments; or paid service providers who work with their own dogs on a contract fee basis.

Team, Group

A visiting dog and handler are considered a team. Several teams working together, or who have formed an organization, are considered a group.

Staff

Staff refers to the people who work for the therapeutic or educational facility where dogs are visiting. Every visitation requires some level of staff support.

Trainers and Instructors

Trainers are crucial to visiting programs. Every visiting dog must learn appropriate behaviors and social skills. The term trainer refers to a person who teaches those skills to a dog. Usually, the trainer is also a dog's handler.

Instructors teach handlers how to train their dogs, how to handle their dogs ethically, and how to visit safely and effectively. For a clearer understanding, throughout this book, instructor refers to the teacher who works with a handler and trainer refers to the person who is actually teaching a dog.

This book's focus is on issues and concepts visiting dogs and handlers must be aware of, and not on specific how-to techniques. That would require another book altogether. Often said of trainers, instructors, and specific training techniques:

"The only thing two trainers will ever agree on is that a third trainer is wrong."

Veterinarians

Every visiting dog must have an annual checkup from a veterinarian who understands the nature of the service the dog provides so that zoonotic concerns (conditions that can be passed between people and animals) are appropriately addressed. Some visiting programs require veterinary care or precautions beyond what is considered the norm for a family pet.

Evaluators, Testers

Organizations that register visiting dogs require that dogs and their handlers successfully meet evaluation or testing criteria. Screening criteria differs from organization to organization, as do the evaluation or tester designation processes. Different organizations use different terms for the people who screen visiting teams, but the terms mean the same thing. For purposes of identification throughout this book, all such people are referred to as evaluators/testers when they are working in an official capacity for a particular organization.

Assessors

This book advocates that visiting dogs' behavior be observed day-to-day and moment-to-moment, and this author advocates that any dog be removed from any environment that might overwhelm that dog. Since the terms "evaluate" and "test" are so readily associated with "evaluators" and "testers" who offer one-time registration evaluations (at best only once every two years, and at not-so-best once in a dog's life time) this author has chosen to use a different set of words to describe a different procedural mindset.

Throughout this book "assessment" refers to what should be a continual process of observing behaviors to determine if a dog is comfortable in a particular environment at a particular time, and "assessor' refers to anyone in a position to determine whether a particular dog should begin or continue visiting. During visits, assessors include handlers, staff overseeing visiting programs, and perhaps group administrators if applicable. Knowledgeable instructors and veterinarians should serve as assessors long before a team ever starts visiting, to provide valuable input to handlers as to a particular dog's suitability for the task. Input received early on serves to encourage handlers to prepare their dogs for visiting programs, or to explore other activities that are better suited to their talents.

Therapy

Therapy refers to a specific treatment of a disease, condition or disorder. In today's health care world of third-party reimbursement, therapy must be prescribed and directed toward meeting specific, documented goals, and therapy must be prescribed and administered by a person with specific credentials and licenses. A dog and handler are not providing "therapy" unless the interactions meet specific criteria.

Modality

Modality refers to a tool or instrument used to elicit a response or achieve results. Visiting dogs are modalities.

Service Dog, Assistance Dog

A dog trained to perform specific tasks for a person with a disability is defined as a service or assistance dog. People who are partnered with service/assistance dogs are granted public access rights by the Americans with Disabilities Act (ADA). Service/assistance dogs are not defined as pets.

Therapy Dog, Visiting Dog

A variety of dogs who work or volunteer, live or visit in a number of settings are currently defined as therapy dogs. Trying to understand the definition is confusing enough, let alone trying to discern which role is being described when one refers to a "therapy dog." Usually the dog's role has very little to do with therapy. "Activity" is often used to describe those interactions that are not by definition therapy, yet no one ever uses the term "activity dog."

An editorial in the September, 2002 International Association of Assistance Dog Partners Partners Forum newsletter states that confusion over public accommodation (for service dogs) is due to the existence of three types of therapy dogs, which the editor describes as:

1. Dogs providing therapy in settings such as hospitals, nursing homes, school and rehabilitation centers;
2. Dogs employed by professional therapists
3. Dogs providing comfort, increased social interactions and relief of stress for a person with disabilities.

This third point signaled a shift in defining dogs who provide emotional support from "service dogs" to "therapy dogs." This is more than a matter of semantics when you consider that only service dogs are allowed the benefit of public access with their humans. On its website in August, 2003, the oldest of the national visiting dog registries, Therapy Dogs, Incorporated, offered its own interpretation of "therapy dog."

"Currently all dogs which are registered with Therapy Dogs International, Inc. provide emotional service only! Laws in various states are confusing and often use the phrase "therapy dogs" to indicate dogs that may or may not be a dog used for emotional service. Laws have to be read carefully as sometimes the legislators are not aware of the difference between an emotional service dog and an assistance dog for people with disabilities. Emotional Service Dogs are the type of dogs which are registered with Therapy Dogs International, Inc."

Currently the Americans with Disabilities Act uses the term "service dog" to identify those non-pet dogs who work with people with disabilities and enjoy public access privileges. No wonder confusion exists.

Other people define puppies and dogs brought into nursing homes and schools from animal shelters and sanctuaries as therapy dogs, and the activity is often referred to as pet therapy. The behavior of these young dogs is not predictable, and the chances that they are enjoying the outing as much as the people they visit, or the people who take them visiting, are questionable.

Some facilities adopt dogs to live on site. These dogs are usually referred to as "resident therapy dogs." As with the puppies, the dogs are seldom assessed or trained for the environment. A better option for all is a visiting program which utilizes trained, assessed teams comprised of competent handlers and appropriate dogs.

To further complicate the name game, schools are not allowed to prescribe "therapy" for students without parental consent, and so schools often oppose the association of the terms "therapy" or "therapy dogs" with dog-related school programs. When this author offered experiential exercises with a trained dog to elementary and high school groups, school counselors did not define our role as a therapy. Instead, our stated goal was to teach social skills to select students.

While many handlers continue to call their visiting dogs "therapy dogs," subtitles are appearing. Programs in public schools that encourage children to read to visiting dogs have proven hugely successful. Dogs that are registered as therapy dogs are renamed "reading dogs" for these programs. Sandi Martin of Utah, who pioneered and launched the concept nationwide, has developed a program called R.E.A.D., which offers another category of visiting dogs that has dropped the term "therapy" and added the term "assistance" within their titles, Reading Education Assistance Dogs.

One of this country's most active community crisis response training organizations, National Organization for Victims Assistance (NOVA) teaches human crisis responders to use terms like "intervention" and "intervener" instead of "therapy" or "therapist" because of liability issues associated with offering therapy. Following September 11, 2001, as media attention was drawn to the hundreds of visiting dogs and their volunteer handlers comforting the most visible victims of a horrific event, people began looking for ways to prepare themselves and their dogs for future crises. New brands of therapy dog designations recently have been introduced, including animal-assisted crisis response, disaster response dogs, and disaster stress-relief dogs. All are visiting teams, the names are meant to imply an elevated, separate status for some visiting teams over others.

The focus of this book is on the issues that surround all

dogs who interact in close proximity with unfamiliar people in any unfamiliar environment. The linguistics associated with various venues is not as important as the ethics associated with the ways the dogs involved are treated.

This book relates to all dogs who live within their human handlers' families and are taken into therapeutic or educational environments to work with people. Since the exact term for what each dog is doing can be confusing and politically challenging, throughout this book, any and all of these dogs will simply be referred to as visiting dogs. They visit the environments in which they work. It's that simple.

Animal-Enhanced Program

Several popular terms refer to the concept of dogs working in human service venues, including pet therapy, pet-facilitated therapy, animal-assisted therapy, animal-assisted activities, and pet visitations. This author believes that appropriate dogs not only assist, they *enhance*, opportunities for people to heal, learn, and improve the quality of their lives. The issues explored in this book are dog-specific and not program-specific, so animal-enhanced program is used throughout as a non-specific reference to *any* program.

Chapter 2
Then and Now

My first opportunity to visit a facility with my dog came unexpectedly and it changed my life.

Some time during the early 1990s, I received a phone call from a nursing home activities director who had found my dog obedience center's listing in the local phone book. She asked me to visit her facility with a trained dog and "do a dog show" (her words) for the residents there. A few evenings later, I reported to the nursing home with Dusty, a snappy red merle Australian Shepherd. After a brief introduction, we proceeded to show those residents how they, too, might achieve great scores in obedience competitions. About twenty elderly folks sat captive in their wheelchairs in a large room, and while my dog and I demonstrated exemplary heeling, half of our audience fell asleep.

My first instincts told me to take Dusty, heel out to my car and disappear, but I worried about the people who were still awake. Surely they'd think it peculiar that their Tuesday evening activity hadn't lasted ten minutes. With one eye on the door, I announced that our introduction had concluded, and now Dusty would like to come around and meet them.

As we approached the group, a yearning in the eyes of an alert man seemed to will us over to his wheelchair. When Dusty wiggled into this man's personal space and put her head in his lap, I observed what I am still only able to describe as "magic." The man smiled, and then he laughed a couple of chuckles, and then he said, "You are so pretty," and began stroking the dog's head with one hand. Not only did this man respond, his infectious enthusiasm prompted the woman dozing in her wheelchair close by to open her eyes. She smiled and gave the order, "Come over here, dog." So it went, again and again, as Dusty moved from person to person. That lethargic environment changed. The room seemed to wake up and become alive.

Since that evening, I have been exploring ways to shape, mold, and redirect that sense of magic to improve the quality of human lives. Now, in a number of ways, my dogs and I work with therapists and educators who incorporate the dogs as tender modalities to enhance rehabilitation, learning, and self-awareness. At the core of each program is the basic magical talent that nature bestows upon some dogs to communicate to people, "Just as you are right now, this moment, I feel a wonderful connection with you. No strings attached, I just want to be close to you." That's a powerful message, most especially when it's delivered during times when people need to hear it most.

Therapeutic, educational, and spiritual relationships with animals have been reported throughout history: animals as gods, animals as demons, animals as religious sacrifices, animals as livelihoods, animals as friends and beloved companions, animals as teammates in sport, animals as liberators to increase the independence of people with disabilities, and animals as modalities to facilitate human learning and healing.

There are very few documented accounts of purposeful therapeutic interventions that included dogs prior to 1960. Some therapeutic accounts of farm animals have been documented in mental health settings in England and Belgium in the early 1800s. In the United States, a visiting animal program at St. Elizabeth's Hospital in Washington, D.C. began in1919, which included dogs, among other animals, in a mental health program.

During the 1960s, psychologist Dr. Boris Levinson began writing about his experiences utilizing his dog, Jingles, in his professional practice. When Levinson surveyed other psychotherapists, he discovered that more than one-third of them had included animals in their work, too.

Prior to the 1970s, documentation points to residential, mostly farm-related animal-enhanced programs, and to professional therapists who brought in animals from outside the environment to interact with their patients. Finally, volunteer organizations emerged, initially made up of people desiring to visit health care facilities with their dogs.

The popularity of visiting with family dogs caught on and grew rapidly in the United States with the incorporation of national organizations that promoted volunteer participation. Three similar registry organizations eventually emerged, offering a sense of approval and volunteers' liability insurance to visiting teams.

Therapy Dogs International, Inc. (TDI) is the oldest registry for visiting dogs in the United States. Elaine Smith, a registered nurse, observed the benefits of visiting pets while she was working in England. When she returned to the United States, she brought with her the concept of dogs visiting special care facilities. In 1976, she founded TDI. The first group of TDI dogs included five German Shepherds and one collie, all titled advanced-level obedience trial competitors.

After the American Kennel Club (AKC) developed the Canine Good Citizen (CGC) Test, TDI adopted the test as their standard for testing and registering visiting dogs. TDI has added additional requirements to the CGC test and TDI requires that the test be administered by an approved TDI evaluator. Once a team has been tested it does not have to test again. TDI evaluator approval is currently based on experience. There are currently no TDI training requirements for handlers or evaluators. In response to the terrorist attacks in New York City, TDI introduced a disaster response test, used to designate teams approved to provide emotional support following disasters.

In 1990, Jack and Ann Butrick founded Therapy Dogs Incorporated, (TDInc.) to register visiting dog teams. The Butricks were formerly members of TDI. To register through TDInc., dog and handler teams must pass one initial test and satisfactorily complete three separate follow-up visits, all overseen by approved TDInc. tester/observers. Just as with TDI, after a team has been tested once, it does not have to test again. TDInc. tester/observer approval is currently based on experience. There are currently no TDInc. training requirements for handlers or tester/observers..

Also in 1990, under the direction of Maureen Fredrickson, an already established Delta Society® developed the Pet Partners® program to register visiting animals. Pet Partners includes most species of domestic animals. Pet Partners registration requirements include successfully completing a skills test loosely based on AKC's Canine Good Citizen test and an accompanying aptitude test given by an approved Pet Partners evaluator. Handlers who register through Pet Partners must either read a home study book or attend a day-long workshop. Teams must be re-evaluated every two years. Currently, evaluators for Delta Society are licensed through that organization, and must complete a home-study book and video and a day-long workshop to qualify.

During the time that these three national visiting dog registries were developing their one-test-fits-all screening standards, the most popular activity for volunteer teams was visiting residents of nursing homes, but that trend is changing rapidly. Growing numbers of professional people – educators and health care providers – are now taking their dogs to work with them as professional modalities. Dogs are volunteering and working in every kind of health care and educational institutions imaginable. Applications include everything from providing company and social connection to interactive goal-directed therapy, experiential education, and crisis response.

The usefulness of dogs in educational and therapeutic environments seems only to be limited by imagination.

In order to meet their own progressing needs, visiting volunteers in communities all across the USA are forming local groups. Some local groups maintain an affiliation with a national organization, but require additional training and screening for participation in their programs. Others have cut national ties and have developed screening, insurance, registration, and administrative policies they feel better meet the needs of their members and the people they serve.

Humans are becoming creative in developing new and innovative ways for dogs to comfort and motivate. As a result, therapeutic and educational applications have progressed in leaps and bounds. However, human capacity to realistically assess the environments in which dogs are being required to work, and to respond ethically to what the dogs are communicating, has not kept pace with these new applications.

Recently, and particularly since September 11, 2001, national organizations and local groups have developed achievement markers based on where dogs visit and the amount of media attention garnered. It seems like the more difficult the environment is for the dogs, the more prestige humans attach to that environment. Human ego and peer pressure have become the new issues with which visiting dogs must contend.

At one time, visiting dogs offered a friendly hello to groups of immobilized individuals in nursing homes. Today, they interact with groups of active children in special education programs and they work at the heart of disaster sites that surely overwhelm their senses, while interacting with people who have been emotionally devastated.

Traditional people cling to established practices; progressive people embrace new concepts. Progressive people have developed new and creative animal-enhanced programs, yet they still rely on traditional, often ineffective, assessment tools. Today, one of the most important challenges facing visiting dogs is human non-awareness of the complex, stressful environments in which the dogs are being required to participate.

Chapter 3
Reciprocity

Dogs seem to have an unpretentious way of attracting media attention. Recently, a television news segment in our area featured an animal-enhanced program at Jim Thorpe Rehabilitation Hospital in Oklahoma City. The stars of this clip were a wonderful volunteer father-and-daughter team and their Labrador Retriever, Rusty. The family had adopted Rusty from a rescue organization and brought him to me for training. After seeing the potential in Rusty and his handlers, I encouraged them to continue their collective education and become a visiting team.

The fact that Rusty has only three legs seemed important to the reporter who put the Jim Thorpe story together. Much of the focus was on the dog's ability to connect with people in a rehabilitation setting because of his perceived disability. The reporter also successfully captured images of Rusty playing at home with his human family, whom he obviously adored. The story reflected a high degree of commitment from a hospital willing to create policies, train staff, and allow volunteer teams into their facility – all to enhance patient services.

This single three-minute clip offered free, positive publicity to a specific hospital, a specific training professional, and non-specific rescue groups. People viewing the story also were introduced to the benefits of having a dog within the family and the benefits to training their dogs. Also covered in the segment were the benefits to patients who are able to connect with visiting dogs, dramatically promoting the concept of animal-enhanced programs in clinical settings and the rewards of volunteering with visiting dogs.

Benefits to Patients and Students

Structured animal-enhanced programs offer facilities and professionals modalities whose usefulness is boundless. One appropriate dog, a skilled handler, and a knowledgeable staff person can develop interactive exercises that reach a broad range of patients, clients or students. A program can be tailored to address virtually any topic or physical condition from a positive, rather than a problem-focused, position. Generally speaking, the best treatments or lessons are those in which the clients or students initiate and participate actively. Appropriate dogs are often on the frontline of successful treatment by encouraging patients or students to participate in a wide variety of specific physical, cognitive, psychosocial, communication and educational goals.

Benefits to Dogs

Every dog needs a job, and when they are appropriately designed, jobs for visiting dogs create positive opportunities for everyone involved, including the dogs. Through training and visiting, dogs gain quality time with their humans. During visits, dogs are the focus of attention.

In addition to the individual rewards received directly by visiting dogs, there are far-reaching benefits that extend to all dogs. As awareness of visiting dogs increases, so does public perception of dogs as valuable partners, deserving the most humane treatment and responsible care. Humane organizations and rescue groups do well by capitalizing on the human service efforts of dogs of mixed breeding, dogs with disabilities, older dogs, or other kinds of "throw-away" dogs, who are sometimes not viewed as good candidates for pets. Visiting dogs are in highly visible positions to highlight the worth of every dog when it is given a chance.

Visiting dogs are models of the well-trained companion. They promote dog training, which benefits all dogs who would otherwise be taken to shelters because of their behavior. Handlers who visit with their dogs lose track of the times patients, students, staff, and family members stare and sigh, "I wish *my* dog behaved like that." That statement presents handlers with countless opportunities to educate people about training. People are often both surprised and motivated to learn that the wonderful dog they are looking at had to be taught this behavior, and was not born this way.

Discussion about the benefits visiting dogs receive and give would be lacking if it did not include dogs who might not enjoy visiting. People can be unaware that not all dogs are suited to the task of being touched, petted and hugged by unfamiliar people in unfamiliar settings. Much more will be discussed throughout this book about the human expectations placed on visiting dogs.

Benefits to Handlers

No matter how much a dog enjoys contact and being petted, and no matter how motivated the patient or student might be to practice their skills, it simply can't happen without an energetic handler. The dog is not going to train himself, bathe himself, jump in the car and drive himself to a nearby school or hospital. Handlers participate in animal-enhanced programs because they benefit, too.

Maybe the most obvious benefit relates to the handlers desire to help people and visiting with their dogs is an enjoyable way for these handlers to feel like they are making important contributions. Another priority for handlers is spending time with their dogs. Visiting, traveling to facilities, training, and preparing all offer quality time together. A priority for some handlers is promoting animal welfare issues or teaching responsible pet ownership, and the example set by a well-behaved visiting dog maximizes those points. Other fringe benefits for handlers include socializing with people, learning new personal growth skills, and learning dog-related skills to enhance interactions.

Some people, who would not otherwise volunteer, do so because of their dogs. Dogs make it easier for the human half of the team to approach unfamiliar people in sometimes awkward circumstances. Everyone's focus is on the dog, not the handler, and topics for conversation are plentiful when a dog is present. Perhaps the least recognized benefit of all is that the dogs often are the enablers that get their human handlers to participate in visiting programs.

Benefits to Facilities and Organizations

Establishing an animal-enhanced program is a detailed process. Administrators must carefully consider policy development to address dog-and-handler selection criteria, infection control issues, patient or student selection criteria, staff training, scheduling issues, and risk management.

In spite of the issues to consider, there are hundreds of well-established animal-enhanced programs all across the United States and other countries, which indicate that the benefits far outweigh the challenges. Schools and health care organizations are learning to enjoy the reciprocal benefits that surround the dogs who visit their institutions.

Positive publicity is not an oxymoron. In today's world of law suits and reports of misconduct, the images of dogs who make a positive difference in the lives of people are as delightful as they are sought after. Positive press and television coverage is worth more than paid advertising in the same media, and visiting dogs invite frequent coverage. Since 1995, dogs I have worked with have been featured seven times on local television stations, with a few of those segments breaking into national markets. My own visiting dogs have appeared in a pilot for a television series about dogs and commercials for health care organizations. Newspaper coverage also has been generous.

Health care is a highly competitive market. Animal-enhanced programs often provide the kind of "bright" or feature story that most marketing personnel can only dream of. Administrators wisely include mention of animal-enhanced programs in promotional and intake materials to attract patients.

Some animal-enhanced programs qualify for grants and can be structured and documented to meet third party reimbursement criteria. Documentation and billing are among the topics more appropriately reserved for professional health care groups.

Benefits to Staff

Staff people can use the connection between themselves and visiting dogs to everyone's benefit. Clients, patients and students are often keenly aware of a visiting dog's happy-to-be-here attitude and link that attitude to a competent staff. "If a dog likes them (the therapist, teacher, counselor), they must be worthy of my attention, too" is the prevailing attitude. Increased cooperation between staff and clients often results, making the staff's job easier and the patient's outlook brighter.

An indirect way to improve patient care is to improve the mood of the staff. The benefits that dogs bring into an environment are not limited to the people receiving care; it also extends to the people *providing* care.

Benefits to Trainers and Instructors

The benefits visiting dogs provide to trainers and instructors are limitless, yet this population, as a whole, seems to be the least aware of potential opportunities. Visiting dogs and their handlers offer dog trainers and instructors everywhere new opportunities to increase clientele, develop new strategies, attract positive publicity, and increase awareness of animal welfare issues.

People who want to develop effective visiting skills with their dogs require knowledgeable trainers and instructors. It is an important role that will be discussed later in this book.

Chapter 4
Roles

It's a good thing Cookie wasn't the dog I originally wanted her to be. She came into my life during a time when I was visiting with a golden retriever who was soon to retire and I was waiting for a young Labrador Retriever to mature. Cookie was a confident, friendly young adult standard poodle in need of a home, and so we became family and soon after that, we became professional partners

It didn't take me long to realize that neither keeping her hair cropped nor referring to her as a curly coated water spaniel would make Cookie into anything she wasn't designed by nature to be. She soared through training and socialization exercises, participating eagerly and enthusiastically, and her first months of work with me in a hospital were stellar. With exemplary skill and her shamelessly solicitous behavior, she was a huge hit. But after a relatively short time, I saw her behavior changing, first as she slowed down or hesitated when greeting some of our patients, and shortly after that, when I read "Do I have to?" in her body language. I removed her from the hospital program and replaced her with the less dynamic, but steady, Labrador Retriever, Scout, who excelled in that environment until his retirement several years later.

Coincidentally, during this same time period, I began exploring avenues for dogs to help special education students develop communication and social skills. I'd researched ropes courses, adventure courses, farm animal and equine programs. It seemed to me that hands-on exercises with dogs could prove equally successful.

We were able to develop some interesting experiential programs, and Cookie and I worked together for the next three years with special education teachers and counselors in three different facilities. Our weekly programs included one semester at an alternative high school program for adjudicated teens, two semesters with elementary school children identified as having learning disabilities, two semesters with elementary school aged children identified as having emotional difficulties, and a ten-week block with a group of elementary school children identified as being at-risk.

We developed programs that taught students to work Cookie through modified obedience exercises while they observed, identified, and discussed Cookie's behavior. When the children communicated their needs appropriately, Cookie responded. When the children communicated in ways that Cookie did not understand, or in ways that confused her, Cookie was free to respond naturally, which helped the child learn to manage their situations. Cookie did not shut down or become anxious as a more sensitive or less secure dog might have. When students stopped to breathe and reorganize, Cookie stopped too, made eye contact and nudged a hand. We called this the "I love you, man" move and each time it happened, a staff person or student from the group would call out, "I love you, man!"

The exercises helped the children meet goals such as effectively communicating, following instructions, sequencing, offering and receiving compliments, and exercising self-control within a group. Preparation and processing led to staff facilitated discussions that focused on a wide variety of topics that related to working with Cookie: overcoming obstacles, causes of stress in dogs, causes of stress in people, signs of stress, calming techniques, body language, personal territory and intimidation, boundaries, how dogs learn, how people learn, how behaviors change, assertiveness without anger, reward and punishment.

Cookie hadn't "fit" into hospital visiting environments, but she thrived in highly active experiential school programs. One job wasn't right for her, but a changed environment changed the dog's behavior. Interestingly, Cookie's national registration was based on an evaluation given in a mirrored room used to teach dance at a community recreation center. The evaluation site resembled neither a hospital nor a public school.

Animal-enhanced programs rely on three primary players: a dog, a handler, and at least one staff person. Sometimes the handler and staff roles are bundled up in the same person, as when educators, counselors, therapists or health care providers work with their own dogs in their professional environments. Trainers and instructors who work with visiting teams assume responsibility for a most vital secondary role.

Since the first national therapy dog registration group formed in the 1970s, all visiting dog and handler teams have earned registration approval or certification based one-time tests or evaluations. Currently, of the three most popular national organizations that register visiting animals, one requires testing every two years, and the two others require only one test in each dog's lifetime. Tests and evaluations are usually set up in non-visiting environments such as dog training facilities (often where the dog has been training for a period of time), gymnasiums, recreation centers or community centers. Currently, this process is considered normal. Normal is, by definition, what most people are doing. Fortunately, normal is always subject to change.

Usually in professional settings, it is only after people have learned a craft or earned a professional degree that they take a test for certification or licensure. Credentialed people then interview for a specific position based on their individual qualifications. Even after being hired, they are assessed on a regular basis within their working environments to measure their levels of competency. It would be preposterous to assume that every doctor, therapist, engineer, or plumber who had once passed a test in an institutional setting would never again be evaluated. Yet people currently make that very same assumption regarding any registered visiting dog and handler team.

Each animal-enhanced program should have job descriptions, and teams should be interviewed to determine their suitability for a specific environment and task. Not only should staff people interview handlers and dogs, but also handlers should actively assess each environment to determine if it seems appropriate for their dog. Handlers must be taught self -assessment skills. Before and during visits, each handler should be self-assessing moment-to-moment. Throughout each visit, a staff person also should be assessing each team. Staff must be taught program assessment skills. Assessments are made through careful observation, not necessarily a formal process, to determine whether a team is in balance with a specific environment. If a team is not able to fulfill its role, either the environment or the team must change.

Although specific criteria will be different, depending on each program's goals and environmental issues, a successful visit depends on how well each player performs his or her specific role. Simply stated:

The handler's role is to present the dog.
The dog's role is to receive the clients (patients, students, residents).
Staff's role is to facilitate the intervention.
A trainer/instructor's role is to prepare the team.

Presenting the dog involves preparation (training, veterinary care, grooming), assessments prior to every visit, moment- to-moment assessments during visits, and being the dog's advocate. Presentation also includes knowledgeable and proactive handling to enhance the dog's ability to best meet the needs of the population being visited, and a basic knowledge of communication skills to enhance human-to-human interactions.

Receiving clients involves a dog's acquired skills and inherent talents, which allow people to perceive that the dog is welcoming them and feels comfortable in their personal space. In order to receive people, the dog must be touchable, reachable, and able to be positioned to best enhance dog-to-human interactions.

It is the staff's job to select appropriate teams and clients, provide appropriate visiting areas, and determine program and individual goals. During visits, staff must be present to facilitate interactions between clients and teams, and to meet any client needs that might arise.

Although preparing the team involves both handler and dog, it is the handler who is responsible for ethical and effective visits. Reputable trainers and instructors launch teams into therapeutic and educational settings, and offer handlers the tools they need to avoid inadvertently overwhelming their canine teammates.

The chapters that follow relate to important issues and concepts that surround ongoing handler, dog, staff, and trainer roles. Programs that place a strong focus on specific jobs and ongoing assessments significantly increase the potential for safe and effective interactions.

Chapter 5
Canine Proxemics and Kinesics

What weighs just four pounds, feels like a soft fluffy cloud, and is modality of choice for many patients in one Oklahoma City rehabilitation hospital? The answer: a Whisper – and this Whisper is no secret. In addition to her work at the hospital, the little Pomeranian has demonstrated her talents at educational programs for nursing students, future therapy dog evaluators, health care providers, and disaster response trainees.

Every week, Whisper teams up with speech, occupational, physical, and recreational therapists during individual therapy sessions. I see her receiving patients, offering much more than a soft touch and pretty face. Children and adults who have had head injuries, spinal cord injuries, strokes, or amputations find Whisper's playful charm hard to resist. Pediatric patients *enjoy* practicing balance and trunk control and increasing their endurance, while playing with Whisper on the floor. Whisper's solicitous antics motivate patients to walk from their wheelchairs to Whisper's table. Speech therapists encourage patients to initiate conversation or recall information about Whisper as she rests in patients' laps. As they practice sensory integration by exploring Whisper's coat of many colors, patients are often unaware *this is therapy!* By sharing enthusiasm and affection, Whisper encourages success. Her confidence seems to be contagious, and the achievements of patients who catch it can be remarkable.

Visiting dogs are not limited to any size, but small dogs like Whisper bring with them unique intrinsic vulnerabilities that I believe are associated with being prey as well as predator. Most wild rabbits weigh more than Whisper. Predators often hover over, swoop in, grab their prey, and carry it off for consumption. I believe that nature has endowed all tiny animals, including dogs like Whisper, with an intuitive sense of the seating arrangement at nature's dinner table. In addition to a sense of the sanctity surrounding personal territory that every dog possesses, I believe Whisper's inner voice alerts her to situations that resemble hovering, swooping, and grabbing. Warranted or not, her body responds to her intuition and I must respond to her signals that indicate she has changed from feeling safe to feeling uncomfortable.

When patients and staff people compare Whisper to my large dogs, I often joke that "Whisper does nothing, but she's trained to do it really well." In reality, Whisper's successes have very little to do with her formal training.

I structure Whisper's working environments carefully. Whisper only works on the floor when her patients and therapists sit (down) on the floor with her. Whisper is positioned on a table (up as high as a human's midsection) to initially greet patients who walk up to her. I place Whisper on her familiar pillow in the laps of already seated patients. They do not pick her up, I do. When therapists or family members stand (hover) over Whisper when she is in the lap of a seated patient, I offer them chairs that I position outside of their arms' length. I've developed friendly, positive ways to reposition people in the environment who are not our patients.

Just as surely as Whisper carries her natural vulnerabilities into the environments in which we work, I am convinced that she trusts that I will always respect her sensitivities. If I were unwilling to respond to her, Whisper's apprehensions ("This can be a scary place") would be confirmed. If that happened, we would lose the confident, solicitous qualities that cause people to feel such a strong connection to her. Every handler can develop a strong, trusting relationship with his or her dog by studying canine language and behavioral patterns, and committing to objectivity regarding the messages their dogs might be sending. The key to keeping enthusiastic visiting dogs from burn out is for handlers to learn these lessons *before* they commit to visiting, and not in the midst of chaos.

Nothing else dogs do compares to the kinds of intrinsically stressful social interaction that takes place when they visit clinical, educational, or post-trauma situations. No other canine-related event, no sport nor competition requires a dog to enter the intimate zones of unfamiliar humans and remain there for several minutes of petting and hugging.

Brief interactions with judges in show rings do not compare to the prolonged and repeated contact that takes place during animal-enhanced programs. Search-and-rescue dogs often work in chaotic environments, but not with prolonged physical contact of unfamiliar people. Service dogs work beautifully in public settings but the public is actively discouraged from touching, petting, and distracting them. Humans have developed a role for visiting dogs like no other in existence. The role is new, specific, and profound.

Most dogs have been bred for generations to distinguish between outsiders and family, and to act accordingly. There has never been a breed of dog designed to enjoy encroachment from strangers. Dogs who actually enjoy interactions in clinical and educational settings are very rare, and the uniqueness of their talent should be appreciated.

Proxemics is the study of personal space and the degree of separation individuals maintain in social situations. Each species has its own rules relating to personal territory. Dogs, including therapy dogs, are no exception.

Within each personal territory, there are zones. The zone at which an individual is first aware of another is the public zone, and it begins when individuals are about twenty-five feet from each other. From there one enters the social zone. Although it is permissible to be in another's social zone, it is the non-verbal communication between the individuals that will make the situation either intimidating or acceptable. Moving still closer brings an individual into another's personal zone, which can be read either as a sign of favor or manipulation.

Closer than the personal is the intimate zone, which ranges from eighteen inches to actual contact. An individual is overwhelmingly aware of another within one's intimate zone. Species maintain rigid rules of communication within this proximity. Ignoring or being unaware of those rules can be perceived as disrespect or intimidation. *(See chart, p. 38)*

In animal-enhanced interventions, people usually walk right into a dog's intimate zone without much introduction. Dogs also are guided into the intimate zones of people in unfamiliar settings – sitting in wheelchairs, lying in beds, standing, or sitting on floors. Whenever the barrier of an intimate zone is crossed, dogs respond by signaling. To the dog, these signals are obvious announcements of respect, appeasement, fear, defensiveness or aggression; yet visiting dogs are routinely required to enter environments where their language is completely foreign. It is up to the handler to interpret and *respond* to the dog's important communiqués.

After an initial human-to-human greeting, a handler usually walks the visiting dog straight up to the person being visited, or the person ambulates straight up to the dog's head. Often the person makes direct eye contact with the dog then touches the top of the dog's head. A straight approach aimed at the head of a dog signals tension from the dog's perspective. Not averting eye contact can signal aggression or disrespect to the dog; yet most meetings between people and dogs begin just this way.

A better greeting would be to approach in an arc, so that the person ends up at the dog's side instead of directly front-to-front. Handlers can reposition their dogs, or suggest that people who are able reposition themselves, so that dogs and people do not end up toe-to-toe. Even with repositioning and moving in an arc, dogs often signal appeasement or discomfort during greetings. A dog might lick his lips or lick the person, avert eye contact, turn his head away, turn his body away, lie down, roll over, or even try to leave.

Touching is the most intimate act of communication. The only act more intimate or intimidating than touching is sex. Touching is an integral part of almost every animal-enhanced intervention and no one would suggest that people stop petting visiting dogs. However, it is crucial that handlers determine whether the dogs being petted are seeking out this intimate contact, or just obediently tolerating an invasion of their personal space.

People hug each other during greetings as signs of affection. Dogs do not. For a dog, to extend front legs over another dog's shoulders is usually an act of domination. From the dog's perspective, hugs can place unfamiliar people in threatening or dominating positions; yet people are often encouraged to hug visiting dogs. During training, handlers should be encouraged to carefully observe a number of dogs, including their own, before and during hugs and interpret the dogs' reactions. Handlers must respect the ways in which their dogs are hardwired differently from humans and learn the language their dogs use to express their perceptions of the moment.

Kinesics is the study of non-verbal communication – body language. There are two elements to any communication: the delivery and the reception of the message. Body language enables any species to send messages, note reception of messages, break through defenses, and avoid conflict.

Humans tend to consider the messages being sent by dogs more carefully than they consider how dogs interpret human body language. Effective teamwork requires handlers who can relate to their dogs' perceptions of what humans are communicating. Handlers who are effective team leaders can communicate with their dogs using body language, but have limited control over the communication being sent out by other people in the environment. It is a perceptive handler who learns how to relay messages of confidence and security to their dogs in any given situation.

The process of communication is complicated and becomes even more so when different species (humans and dogs in this case) have different interpretations for the signals included in the vocabulary of body language. Although each dog is different, some of the more common dog-related signals concerning personal territory include head turning, lowering head, turning away, averting eye contact, squinting or blinking eyes, licking lips, licking other individuals, grooming, scratching, sniffing, yawning, moving slowly, moving in an arc, moving straight in, sitting, lying down, rolling over, freezing, shaking off, tail wagging, bowing, lifting paws, or raising hackles. Often humans do not recognize these signals or misinterpret them as disinterest or disobedience; yet each signal is part of a message a dog might be trying to convey about personal territory.

During visits that take place in dogs' intimate zones, dogs are likely to communicate respect or appeasement. These "calming signals" include behaviors such as licking their lips, licking people, averting eye contact, turning their heads away, turning their bodies away, lying down, or rolling over. Calming signals are meant to convey, "I know that we are in each other's territory, but don't worry, I mean you no harm."

Sometimes dogs signal respect or appeasement by engaging themselves in activities that have nothing to do with the strangers in their territory. These behaviors, often called "displacement signals," include sniffing the ground, self-grooming, scratching, or perhaps chewing on something. Displacement signals are meant to convey, "We are here in this same territory, but don't be angry. I am not acknowledging you. See? I am totally doing something else." Doing something else also seems to lessen the stress associated with dogs' perceptions of inappropriate social contact. Handlers who do not understand the communication taking place often punish these types of displacement behaviors. Over time, if corrected consistently, dogs stop communicating in this way. Their discomfort remains, but their observable indicators disappear, making these dogs' future behavior much harder to predict.

Dogs also communicate fear. People usually don't expect to see fearful or aggressive dogs in visiting situations. Objectivity requires being open to that possibility. Dogs' fears must be acknowledged early on or those fears can escalate into behaviors that look like aggression to humans. Dogs often use barks and growls to convey fear. "You are in my territory and I am afraid. Move away!" It is easy enough for most people to believe that cornered or trapped dogs might react strongly out of fear, but people often don't recognize that trained dogs perceive that they are trapped when they are on leash or when they have been told to stay. Leaving is not an option for them. The perception of being trapped leaves fearful dogs few options other than expressing, "Move away!"

In order to remove any perception of being cornered, visiting dogs can be trained in ways that make it clear to them that it's acceptable to signal discomfort and, if they feel they must move away, their handlers will accommodate them.

Assessing dogs for specific environments is an art that involves keen human observational skills. If assessors and handlers learn to interpret a dog's signaling within the context of the dog's interactions, they will be able to identify the dog's comfort level.

Handlers need to be advocates and interpreters for their non-verbal partners. Instructors are responsible for equipping their handler clients with a thorough knowledge of causes and symptoms of stress in dogs, as well as an understanding of canine body language. Staff people have an obligation to learn to recognize the difference between a confident and comfortable dog, and one whose behaviors reflect intimidation or disinterest. Staff shoulder the final responsibility for removing any team whose behavior might pose a risk to either their clients or the visiting dog.

Even under the best of circumstances, visiting dogs have stressful jobs. Stress is not a dirty word. It is merely the body's way of coping with changes or demands in the environment. Handlers must realize that visiting environments are stressful if only because they represent a huge shift from the dog's normal territory. Prolonged or frequent periods of stress produce anxiety. When any individual is in a state of anxiety, normal thinking stops. To unskilled observers, anxious dogs often appear to be disobedient dogs.

Even those environments most humans consider "easy" bombard the senses of visiting dogs. Handlers often say, "We are just visiting in nursing homes." Consider from a dog's perspective the strong and unusual body, medicinal and chemical odors. Consider the confusing sounds of differing voices and tones, overhead announcements, equipment rolling and pumping, vacuum cleaners and maintenance tools. Consider unknown and potentially threatening areas of dark and light, elevators, stairs, doors that move on their own, uncomfortably high room temperatures, and the peculiar texture of the floor, carpet, or tile underfoot. Against this backdrop, imagine encountering groups of unfamiliar people, who reach out and grab, wanting to touch and hug, all the while moving in and out of the dog's intimate zone.

As if this weren't enough, dogs also are expected to tolerate threatening communication from other visiting dogs, handler behaviors that are inconsistent with what a dog is used to, expectations that are too high for the dog in the moment, pain, thirst, or the need for a bathroom break.

Individual behaviors will vary, but general signs of stress include changes in communication patterns and nonspecific body complaints. Shifts in canine communication patterns are detected through posture, body movement, head movement, and eye movement. Nonspecific body complaints that indicate stress reactions include sweating paws, salivating, panting, yawning, shaking off, sudden loss of hair, restlessness, withdrawal, muscle tenseness, suspiciousness, aggression, hyper-alertness, intensified startle reflex, ducking behind handler, self-mutilation, change in activity, or loss of appetite. Some additional indications of sensory overload include regression or returning to earlier behaviors that had been outgrown, abnormal fear of separation from handlers, or distrust of unfamiliar people.

People seem to be able to recognize canine behaviors that relate to flight or fight as being stress-related more easily than they recognize those stress-related symptoms that indicate a dog is shutting down or freezing. Stress symptoms expressed through increases in activity are referred to as positive stress symptoms, and stress symptoms expressed through decreases in activity are referred to as negative stress symptoms. Handlers sometimes remark that their dogs are "so much more laid back" or "so much calmer" when their dogs are visiting. The key word is "more," denoting a change from the norm. Because behaviors that relate to the expression of negative stress are actually beneficial to visiting environments (calmer, quieter), it is easy for handlers and staff people to overlook what is really happening.

Ethical handlers develop time frames and environmental policies that allow their dogs to visit only within environments that are comfortable for them, and they leave before, not after, their dogs develop major symptoms of stress. Savvy handlers continually watch for the subtle signals their dogs so freely offer and respect the communication by making adjustments, or leaving the environment.

Proxemics
Personal Territory

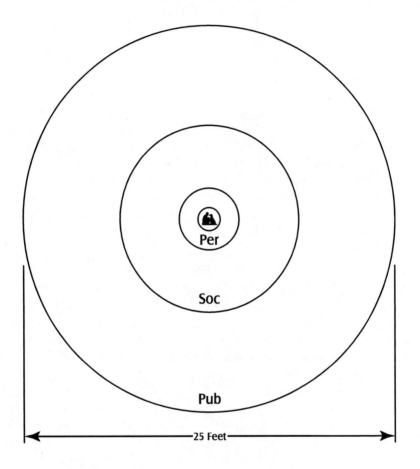

- **Intimate Zone** - 18 inches to contact
Per - Personal Zone - 4 feet to 18 inches
Soc - Social Zone - 12 feet to 4 feet
Pub - Public Zone - 25 feet to 12 feet

Chapter 6
Fundamental Behavior

The most commonly referred to setting for visiting dogs is the nursing home. Most handlers start out by offering meet-and-greet sessions with their dogs to residents of a nearby long- term care facility. I did, too. My first regular gig was with my golden retriever, Partner, volunteering twice a month at a residential veterans' center in my town.

During the same time frame when Partner and I were developing a relationship with our veteran friends, I began taking him to a church youth program. I'd like to say the dog-related spiritual activates were part of my master plan, but more likely it was *my* Master's plan to get me on a path I am still following today. I can see now that I learned a lot about developing experiential education at that church with Partner. Back then I was just trying to keep a small group of young children and a couple of teenage assistants actively engaged. My son and daughter were enrolled in Youth Club at our church on Wednesday evenings. To do my part, I helped with activities, about 45 minutes devoted to fun and fellowship. My group included up to six first- and second-grade children. I took Partner about once a month. Other weeks I fumbled through crafts or games. Partner worked with me at church, off and on, for about three years.

Sometimes our small group sat on the floor, petting or brushing Partner, discussing how we'd been created and how

Partner had been created, our similarities and differences. Partner's big golden head would fill up an entire six-year-old lap as, one by one, they took turns at "holding" the dog while they spoke. I learned that some people like to pet and nurture while they talk, and others prefer to brush and perform functional tasks. I learned that the best thing Partner did was not perform any of his skilled activities; but rather the way he made the children feel simply by getting down on their level and gazing into their eyes while they spoke. He "received" them.

The children also loved that Partner would "do things" for them. We developed "The Tennis Ball Game," which included tiny pictures of crosses, arks, mangers, and stars taped individually to tennis balls. Each child identified one of the pictures, and gave the group an explanation or story about the picture. Then the child removed the picture, threw the ball and gave Partner the cue to retrieve. That game taught me that deep discussions can center on anything you want to stick on a tennis ball.

The bandana game was another favorite of everyone, including Partner. Each child, usually giggling, sat on the floor behind one of six large bandanas. A child would hide a soft training bumper under one of the bandanas while Partner turned his back so he could not see. I had painted a face and sewn red yarn hair on the bumper we used, naming it Baby Bumper, to enhance the game. The other children tried to make their bandanas look as though Baby were hiding there, too.

They got creative and used items like their shoes and socks trying to fool the dog. After the children got the bandanas just right, they collectively called Partner, who walked among the six bandanas until he found Baby Bumper with his nose, picked it up, and delivered it to me. After cheers and applause, discussion came easily, often relating to search and rescue dogs, lost and found, worthiness, uniqueness, and profound love.

During Youth Club, high school-aged members of our church served as teachers' helpers. From the teens assigned to our group, I learned that what works well for children and visiting dogs also works well for teens. I intended for the teens to be involved in a more adult-like role with Partner, but they enjoyed the games so much that they usually did not differentiate themselves from the younger children during these activities. The teenagers taught me that interactions with an appropriate visiting dog can bring out the inner child in almost everyone.

Back then, I learned how Partner's behavior effectively drew the children in and helped them feel safe about expressing their ideas. These early experiences were validated by experts years later as I explored ropes and adventure courses as models for new experiential programs to wrap my dogs around. Partner and Youth Club taught me ways to develop and deliver similar exercises and games for teachers and counselors in special education programs. Now, with different student goals come different discussions and processing, and I am working with different dogs. I presented Partner in a manner consistent with meeting the goals of the church program and Partner received the children in a manner that encouraged participation. I believe the fundamental canine and handler behaviors that enhanced a church-based program back then are the same behaviors that are needed today to enhance the many settings that include visiting dogs.

Today there seem to be no unusual settings for visiting dogs. Hospitals, addiction recovery centers, mental health wards, correction facilities, special education programs, doctors' and dentists' offices, court-related interview sessions, women's shelters, and juvenile detention centers are just a few of the places where dogs have been brought in to enhance healing or learning.

Unfortunately, the methods most people use to determine whether dogs are contributing to the therapeutic or educational process haven't changed much since the 1970s. In fact, no one gives as much attention to whether the dogs are actually enhancing or hindering the process, as much as they consider whether dogs have passed a test or evaluation at some point in their lives. A far more effective policy would be to conduct on-site assessments of each dog and handler in the environment they visit. Cookie-cutter tools are not appropriate for on-site assessments. Assessment tools should be individualized to determine whether teams' behaviors are appropriate for each visiting program in the environment in which that program is being delivered.

Some standard concepts can be applied to every visiting process. Effective visiting processes consist of handlers who appropriately present their dogs and dogs who appropriately receive the people being visited. There are observable, identifiable behaviors that enhance the visiting process and there are behaviors that hinder or reduce the value of the visiting process.

The goals of visiting programs might be therapeutic in nature or they might be educational in nature, or both. Dogs facilitate healing and learning when they contribute to feelings of safety, comfort, and connection. The behaviors that are required to make people feel safe, comfortable, and connected to the dogs who visit them remain consistent. However, dogs' and handlers' abilities to demonstrate specific behaviors depend on environmental factors, as well as team skills and talents. Again, the best way to determine if teams are appropriate for specific environments is by assessing their behaviors within those environments.

Every visiting dog's role is to "receive" the person or people with whom the dog is interacting. The process of being received is what gives people the perception that there is a connection or bond between themselves and the dog. It is primarily that perception which motivates people to participate in therapy, learning, discussion, or other targeted activities.

There is another connection to consider. The perception of a strong moment-to- moment connection between the handler and the dog increases everyone's confidence in the team. Handlers who talk to their dogs in normal everyday tones and who make contact, either by touching or speaking, with their dogs frequently, demonstrate the bond that exists between themselves and their dogs. Every handler should develop skills that reflect a loving partnership with their dog, while subtly suggesting that the handler is indeed the leader and could easily redirect the dog's behavior if necessary.

Specific identifiable canine behaviors tend to enhance the perception of a bond between the dog and the people being visited. Initiating physical contact, staying engaged, making eye contact, respecting personal boundaries, and allowing their behaviors to be redirected all suggest connection.

Canine behaviors that reduce the perception of a bond and hinder the visiting process include disinterest, reluctance to engage, disregard for personal boundaries, and any conduct that might be interpreted as aggressive or stress-related.

It seems preposterous to consider visiting with any dog or accepting dogs into visiting programs, who will not demonstrate a desire to initiate and maintain contact with unfamiliar people; yet it is common for people to regard high levels of canine skill more highly than their desire to engage. The first question handlers should address is whether their dog wants to visit. Currently, most tests and evaluations for registration of visiting dogs do not include any simple "step back and ask the dog" exercise. Evaluators and testers approach the dogs and touch them all over. They surround the dogs with people who reach in and pet, but they never ask the dogs if the dogs themselves would choose to engage if given a choice. The answer is far too important not to ask the question.

During on-site assessments, evaluators can ask dogs this important question by simply stepping back several times throughout the assessment and informally beckoning the dog. When invited, but not being ordered by their handlers, dogs who enjoy visiting with unfamiliar people will initiate contact with their assessors at different times throughout the evaluation. Dogs who are comfortable and enjoy unfamiliar people will remain engaged with their assessors and will offer at least some eye contact.

Conversely, dogs who are not willing to initiate contact or remain engaged with their assessors probably do not want to be touched and petted by unfamiliar people. Certainly, dogs who slide behind their handlers or move toward distractions, away from their assessors, do not demonstrate appropriate behaviors for visiting.

While friendliness and confidence are necessary qualities, visiting dogs must also respect personal boundaries. Dogs must wait for permission before initiating contact. Jumping, pawing, and licking (beyond the few quick and respectful face-to-face calming licks) can seem intrusive to people being visited. It's true some people love "dog kisses," but most people do not.

Dogs who demonstrate behaviors that can be interpreted as aggressive should not visit. Sometimes rumbles and moans are misinterpreted as growls; and sometimes handlers identify growls as rumbles and moans. Some dogs bark when they are excited. Barking dogs may be friendly to a fault, but people being visited will not feel safe if they interpret barking as a threatening behavior. The reasons behind a visiting dog's behavior are not as important as the effects of that behavior on the people being visited.

Behaviors that can be redirected or interrupted give people a greater sense of connection and control. Simply being able to cause a dog to make eye contact by saying the dog's name is enough to create the sense that a connection has been made. The more advanced the dog's abilities are to respond appropriately to the patient, the greater the rewards of the visit.

Most symptoms of stress are universal. People know stress when they see it, even in other species. Not only is it risky and abusive to visit with a dog who is stressing, but the people being visited will recognize the behaviors and ascertain that the dog does not wish to visit with them.

Handlers make up fifty percent of visiting teams, but carry one hundred percent of team responsibility for the visiting process. Important handler behaviors that enhance the value of the visit include pro-active handling skills, being strong advocates for their dogs, objectivity toward their dogs, and good people skills.

Pro-active handlers anticipate their dogs' behaviors and direct their dogs according to what is about to happen. Re-active handlers correct and redirect their dogs after a behavior has occurred. Pro-active handlers make visiting look smooth and easy. Re-active handlers appear always to be working their dogs. Dogs are more comfortable when their handlers behave pro-actively.

There is a strong social connection between handlers and their visiting dogs. The dogs, after all, hold the admission tickets to activities their handlers enjoy very much. It's understandable that some handlers measure a degree of their worth based on the recognition they receive from their dog-related services. Sometimes handlers want to keep the team intact, even when the dog is ready to break up the act. Denial keeps handlers from accepting the unwanted reality that their dogs simply do not enjoy visiting, so handlers offer excuses. They rationalize, they minimize, and they justify their dogs' behaviors. By definition an excuse is intended to remove any blame from a behavior. "Yes, but…"

Handlers who rationalize want their dogs' behaviors to seem justifiable. They offer plausible reasons for their dogs' actions.

"We adopted him from the shelter so he must have been abused. It took him awhile, but now he loves to sit on the floor with our kids. He loves their attention. He probably only tried to leave today because there were too many adults in the room."

Handlers who minimize their dogs' behavior underestimate the impact of the actions on the people they are visiting.

"Well, sure you heard something, but he's a Rottweiler, and Rottweilers rumble. He's not growling, it's just his way of talking. It's no big thing, if you knew anything about dogs, you'd understand that."

Handlers who offer excuses seek to justify the dog's behavior.

"He's not usually this way, but you kept us waiting. He was so excited because he loves visiting, and then he had to sit in your waiting room. When he finally saw you, he couldn't help himself, and he just jumped all over you."

A key issue relating to visiting dogs is that the reasons behind their behavior are not as important as the *effects* of their behaviors. Understanding why a dog reacts in a certain way will not make that dog any more appropriate for visiting programs. Besides, when someone offers excuses for any behavior, it's usually a sign the person is aware that something is amiss.

Some canine behaviors are unique to the task of visiting. Canine competitors are considered to be extremely well socialized because of chaotic environment in which they perform; yet they never experience people petting them all over in the show ring. People often assume incorrectly that these dogs' high levels of performance skills make them automatic candidates for visiting programs.

Another misconception is that all dogs who pass the American Kennel Club's Canine Good Citizen Test will make good visitors. Dogs who demonstrate admirable social skills in public do not always rise to the challenges of visitation. There are also many canine companions who adore the attention of their human family members, but are reluctant to interact with unfamiliar people. Some dogs enjoy company at home, but are not comfortable in settings away from home. A lot of wonderful dogs are simply better suited to something other than visiting programs.

This author believes that dogs and handlers who possess and demonstrate those unique and necessary traits described in this chapter have a "talent" for the task of visiting. Talents are abilities given by nature. There are strong mixed opinions regarding whether reluctant dogs can be trained or conditioned or socialized to a degree where they actually enjoy contact with unfamiliar people in unfamiliar settings. Some dogs who were clearly not appropriate at some stage in their lives have become nice visiting dogs later on. Perhaps they needed help in gaining more confidence or they just needed more maturity and self-control, or they needed gradual exposure to different settings. Other dogs seem intrinsically unable to adjust to the demands of visiting programs.

Chapter 7
Workforce Principles

A handler and her small dog came to an evaluation I was facilitating. They needed this evaluation in order to renew their existing registration. The dog was well behaved, but throughout the evaluation she would not interact with me. In fact, she actively disengaged at every opportunity. I even tried holding her in my lap, but she struggled to jump down. She couldn't have communicated more clearly that she did not want to visit with me.

Following the evaluation, the handler tried in vain to convince me that I should recommend the team for registration. Her flawed logic centered on the importance of their participation at the facility they visited. She used staff's appreciation for a small dog at this particular facility as justification. Her dog was important because she was small enough to be placed and held anywhere to accommodate a challenging population.

The handler showed me a newspaper article about a volunteer's award the team had won and she also had a video. She asked me to keep the video, to see for myself the extraordinary services her little dog offered to the people they visited.

The next day, I watched as much of the video as I could bear, feeling as though I were caught in a risk manager's nightmare. It seemed like so many things that could go wrong in systems that approve visiting dogs were appearing before my very eyes. Young adults with profound developmental disabilities sat in a noisy room with a television blaring. One or two staff members and the handler stood, encircling the little dog as she was placed in each patient's lap or on a lap tray. Most patients seemed to be nonverbal but many did make sounds, sometimes loudly. Some of the patients' heads bounced up and down, almost banging the dog. Staff manipulated patients' hands to help them clumsily pet the dog, who was not much larger than the patients' hands. All the while, throughout each visit, one of the handler's hands remained locked around the dog's hips, holding the dog in place. Clearly, the little dog turned her head away, licked her lips, and her eyes bulged. Just as clearly she stood up and tried to leave, only to be repositioned and held more firmly in place by her handler's clamped hand so that a patient might continue petting. Then, after a minute or two the entourage would move on to another patient and repeat the process.

After watching the video, I telephoned the handler and shared my observations with her. I offered to help her develop new visiting skills that might enable her little dog to feel comfortable again in a different environment. The handler declined.

Later, I received a pleasant note from the handler, thanking me for my time and saying she felt as though neither the registering organization I was representing nor I understood the need for her little dog. She reiterated staff's appreciation for her small, position-able dog, and she told me that she and her dog would continue to visit there. Sadly, the word "visit" hardly seemed appropriate.

In the past few years, workforce management personnel and public school administrators have become increasingly on heightened alert. Identifying and mitigating risks associated with potentially dangerous employees and dangerous students are priorities in this country. Experts define "violence" as an event that has happened, while "safety" refers to prevention. The common threads found in workforce safety programs include screening, training, and planned management. Attorneys who address workforce safety issues emphasize organizational liabilities as well. As workforce safety policies become accepted facts of life, it is surprising that facilities rarely apply the same principles to visiting dog and handler teams.

No one considers visiting dogs or their handlers to be violent creatures, intent on reigning terror wherever they go. However, lack of intent to do harm does not negate the risks associated with visiting animal programs. Some animal-related risks include the transmission of diseases and parasites, dog-related injuries, and damage to facilities and equipment. Handlers also bring elements of risk into visiting environments with improper health and hygiene, breaches in confidentiality, and inappropriate interactions.

Even though visiting teams may carry personal liability insurance, facilities cannot surrender liability issues to the handler. Facilities shoulder primary legal responsibilities for their employees and volunteers. Welcoming dogs and handlers into clinical and educational environments without first assessing the teams' qualifications and behaviors on-site is an unacceptable risk.

Facility administrators are usually not aware of the registration or certification processes that surround visiting teams. Often administrators welcome the news that the teams use "certified therapy dogs," yet those administrators would be hard pressed to describe what "certified therapy dogs" are.

Risk assessors define "safe" as meaning freedom from unacceptable risk. There would probably be no safe activities, if "safe" had to mean freedom from all risk. The challenge is to define what acceptable risk is, and how to deal with it. For example, rabies is always fatal to humans who contract the disease and do not receive treatment. Contact with dogs would be an unacceptable risk to take, except that dogs can be vaccinated to prevent them from contracting the disease and passing the rabies virus. Maintaining current records to prove that visiting dogs have been appropriately vaccinated mitigates a high-stakes risk and makes it acceptable.

There are two kinds of risk-reduction programs: those developed to make people feel safe and those that actually reduce risk. The policies and promotional materials of national organizations that register visiting teams tend to offer facilities and handlers a sense of safety. Handlers assume that, because they have passed a team evaluation and received the approval of a national registration organization, they are equipped to visit safely and effectively in any kind of environment.

People who test and evaluate dogs for registration through national organizations are predicting whether teams will be free from unacceptable levels of risk for years to come, and whether teams will be able to interact successfully with unspecified populations in unspecified environments. The points that people must consider when giving worth to a prediction such as this include the strategic position of the person making the prediction, the experience and knowledge of the person making the prediction, the direct value of the outcome to the person making the prediction, the timing of the prediction, and the availability of reliable indicators.

Tests must be relevant. People who make predictions must observe behaviors in the same environment where visits will take place. Assessments should measure the relationship between the individuals and their environments. Most visiting teams are evaluated by someone in a training center or gymnasium far removed from the clinical or educational environment in which the team will visit. When they are visiting, handlers are in the best strategic positions to observe their dogs' reactions moment to moment and to predict what will happen next. Staff people are also in strategic positions to observe and assess behaviors throughout visits, but they first must understand canine signaling to assess teams effectively.

Health care professionals are invested in the safety of

their clients and, with appropriate training, can make careful predictions regarding teams who visit in their facilities. Handlers are invested in their dogs' well-being; however, handlers must guard against becoming emotionally invested in the outcomes.

The timing of any prediction is critical. Assessors must ask themselves, "Will this team provide safe interactions this day, this moment, this place?" That is a reasonable prediction. Visiting animal tests and evaluations are typically made only once in each dog's lifetime, although one national organization requires re-evaluating every two years. Predictions made years ago are of little value.

A prediction is an estimate of future possibilities based on current trends. In order to predict any outcome, reliable indicators must be available and assessors must know how to read them. Among the important things to consider when predicting the safety of a visiting team are the levels of stress being demonstrated by the dog at any time during the visit, the degree of willingness of the dog to interact, and the ability of the handler to deal with the dog and the environment. The specific behaviors referred to in this paragraph are described in detail in chapters five and six. People can't assess visiting dogs unless they know the indicators associated with enthusiastic and comfortable dogs versus the indicators associated with stressed, fearful, or reluctant participants.

The best way to bring animal-enhanced programs into compliance with current workplace standards is to view visiting teams as part of the workforce for which facilities are responsible. The three areas consistently advocated in risk reduction policies in the workplace are training, planned management, and thorough screening.

Training is a critical component of any prevention strategy. Workforce training involves teaching interviewers to be more skilled and thorough, getting employees to recognize early signs of stress, and encouraging effective communication. Staff people must receive training to understand key points regarding visiting teams, and be able to interview and screen effectively. Staff should be able to identify handler behaviors that enhance or reduce therapeutic value, as mentioned in chapter six.

Handlers should be provided with training that enables them to communicate effectively and interact safely with specific populations. Training must emphasize the important and broad issues of confidentiality and patient and student rights. The only way for staff to know whether handlers have received sufficient levels of training in these areas is to interview them prior to their first visit.

Both staff and handlers should receive incident response training: what defines an "incident" and what to do if one occurs. In addition, staff must be able to identify stress early on, both in dogs and people. Dangerous behavior is a progression that begins before one specific act. Early identification is vital.

Planned management means developing effective policies. There is no reason for facilities to exclude visiting animals and handlers from established workforce procedures. Just as with other workforce criteria, visiting animal and handler policies should include screening and training requirements, infection control, record keeping, planned re-evaluation and review processes, and procedures for counseling, suspension or removal.

Workforce screening policies call for careful pre-employment testing. Administrators must develop assessment processes for visiting teams that take place in the environments in which each team is going to visit. Workplace assessment considers both the individual (team) and the environment. Pre-employment screening should assess fitness for a specific duty.

Professional organizations are legally responsible to mitigate risk in accordance with their own standards of practice. Regardless of "therapy dog certifications" touted by handlers, it is each facility's responsibility to develop policies, training, and screening criteria to determine whether or not each visiting team meets that organization's standards for safety.

Chapter 8
Balance Matters

On the evening of May 3, 1999, the strongest winds ever recorded on this planet ripped through the Oklahoma City area. The tornado stunned the state, leaving destruction and trauma behind. Forty-four people were killed, hundreds more critically or seriously injured. More than 3,000 homes were destroyed, an additional 4,866 homes were declared unlivable. People did not know if injured family members would survive. Families did not know where they would live.

The day after the tornado, central Oklahoma became a well-organized crisis response machine, able to meet the immediate physical needs of each victim. Churches became shelters for the community's newest homeless people. Churches also served as feeding stations and daycare centers for families who spent their daytime hours sifting through rubble and waiting for authorities to validate claims for assistance.

Sherry Gibson, who regularly volunteered with her dog in a special education program, called me on May 5 and asked how she and other handlers might respond. There was no protocol then for taking dogs to comfort people who had recently been through a natural disaster, so after we considered our options, we targeted a church which had been designated as a makeshift daycare center. Young children there were being cared for by community volunteers.

We developed a trio of teams that included Sherry and her golden retriever, Sunny; Barbara Hamon and her pug, Otis; and Pomeranian King Tut and me. I opted for the smallest of my available experienced dogs for this assignment. I was aware, too, that King Tut was also my most vulnerable dog. The three of us and our dogs met up at a central location, and then loaded into Sherry's van to make the arduous journey around the devastated areas of our community to the designated church. We arrived, unannounced, to an enthusiastic welcome from volunteers at the church. They escorted us to a large playroom, which held about seven children who ranged in age from about two to eight years old. Older children were out, sifting through the rubble of their home sites with the adults, and the infants were in a separate room of the church.

The children left at the church were in the last place they wanted to be: a strange building with strange people, absent parents, no familiar toys or stuffed animals, no security blankets – these special items were gone. They had no idea why or how long they would be left at the church. Life had suddenly become very complicated. One child after another stated that their houses were gone. One said that his dog had died. Some could not stop talking. One child bounced around the room in continuous hyperactivity, while another sat eerily motionless in a volunteer's lap.

These children were not ill in the tradition sense, so medicine would not have helped. A different kind of healing was needed, and the dogs moved in as though they knew their work had begun. After a quick assessment of the room, we spread out to different areas, and dropped to the floor, where our dogs could best receive this population.

During the first few minutes, the children bounced in and out of small circles around the dogs, their anxious energy filling up the room. Some children spoke, and we responded briefly; but mostly we allowed our teammates' quiet magic to begin its work. Sunny rested her head in a lap, which motivated that child to focus on petting the dog's soft clean fur. Otis was a snorting pug and when he had walked in, he had attracted everyone's attention. Then he lay still, which encouraged a child to focus on exploring his saggy baggy pug skin. It worked. King Tut found the lap of a child sitting in front of us and hopped in. The child focused on running her fingers through King Tut's long coat and she giggled each time he looked up into her eyes. Another child sat down beside us.

The three dogs received the young people they were visiting, each dog in his and her own way. We handlers presented our dogs specifically and appropriately for the population we were visiting, and the volunteer staff became totally involved in actively facilitating this unique intervention.

As the children petted the dogs, the environment seemed to change. A high-pitched, anxious little boy's voice became normal, and then quiet. A tired child, who had rocked compulsively back and forth, lay down on his side and rested peacefully. Eventually, every bit of hyperactivity came to rest. Everyone in the room seemed to relax, and soon it felt peaceful there. Some adults who were volunteering in other areas of the church came in and sat on the floor, not disturbing the children or touching the dogs, just being in the room with them.

We stayed until parents arrived to pick up their children. The atmosphere seemed to change again, as the children responded emotionally to seeing their parents. It seemed like the right time for us to get back to our families, too.

Three handlers with three dogs entered into an unfamiliar environment with a goal of comforting young children who had lost nearly everything. Mission accomplished. The success of this intervention might best be measured by the positive observable changes in the children's behavior. Success was dependent on the teams' levels of talent, skill and comfort being strong enough to compensate for an unpredictable, emotionally charged environment. Success was a matter of balance.

Everything I ever needed to know about balance and compensation, I learned on the playground. With a teeter-totter for a teacher, young children quickly figure out that it's not just size and strength that matter. The key to success on a teeter-totter lies in the ability and willingness of participants to compensate to achieve balance.

Animal-enhanced programs should be viewed within the context of balance and compensation, too. The participants in any animal-enhanced intervention include the dog and handler as a team on one end of the scale and the environment on the other. When teams and environments are in balance, interventions can reasonably be expected to succeed.

Compensation can be viewed as either adding an equivalent to one side or offsetting an undesired effect. Ethical handlers are prepared to compensate or, if necessary, to walk away any time the environment is stacked against the team.

Team Elements

Although they work together as a team, each handler and dog comes with individual levels of comfort, talent, skill, experience, and confidence in each other. Each team performs its own balancing act between the dog and handler on its end of the balance scale.

Comfort

Comfort levels are dependent on each team member's individual ability to cope with the environment. Comfort levels can vary greatly between the dog and the handler, usually to the dog's detriment. Comfort is mostly a dog-related issue, simply because handlers do not repeatedly take the team into environments where the handler feels uncomfortable.

Sometimes maintaining acceptable comfort levels can be achieved through compensation. A dog might possess a talent for visiting, and feel completely at ease listening to a child read out loud. Yet it is possible for the same dog to be uncomfortable visiting with groups of people or walking through crowded halls. An example of compensating might be to walk through the school once the students were in class, or if the dog were small, to use a carrier. Sometimes choosing a different environment is the only ethical way to achieve and maintain comfort.

Skill and Talent

The most essential element a dog and handler possess is talent, yet it is often overlooked. Talent is a natural endowment. Some people are talented piano players; others simply play the piano. Some dogs are talented agility athletes; others simply complete the obstacles. The behaviors that reflect talent for animal-enhanced programs are those same behaviors that enhance therapeutic and educational value. Talented handlers are able to deal with the reality of their current situation and act as their dogs' advocates. (Dog and handler skills are discussed in detail in Chapter 9.)

Regardless of any team's ability to meet or exceed skill requirements, high levels of skill do not compensate for absence of talent. Talented teams can visit in some settings without high levels of skill. Teams who lack visiting talent should not visit anywhere.

A trend has developed among handlers and groups to bombard visiting canine candidates with stimuli such as overwhelming noises (sirens, horns), irritating odors (cleaning solutions, perfumes), staged human emotional outbursts, and crowded conditions (many teams crammed into transport vehicles). Some people call this "training" and dogs who learn to override their natural inclinations to avoid sensory abuse are deemed "appropriate" for disaster and crisis response.

For dogs, the effects of real human emotion, the stress of having large numbers of unfamiliar humans grabbing and hugging them, contact with toxic surfaces, and overcoming sensory stimuli are not simple training issues. These are humane issues. Certainly, dogs can be trained to persevere in spite of distractions and sensory bombardment. Sadly, the conditioning process inadvertently teaches these dogs not to use calming signals, and less savvy handlers and evaluators mistake the lack of signaling for "being comfortable with." Training dogs to override and endure is better defined as "masking" than "compensating." Just because some dogs are willing to tolerate overwhelming environments does not mean people have license to exploit their visiting partners. Some environments impose too much upon dogs.

Experience, Confidence, Trust
Past experience tells individuals what to expect next. Experience is the teacher that causes dogs and handlers to anticipate visiting with either positive or negative expectations. It is important to note that a dog's perception can differ greatly from a human's perception of the very same event.

Positive experiences produce confidence and trust. Negative experiences produce apprehension and fear. Handlers who protect their dogs from undo stress increase their dogs' confidence. Successes breed confidence, and confidence encourages continued growth. A dog's level of confidence in the handler is based both on their lifelong relationship and how the dog perceives the handler's behavior in the moment. Sometimes nervous, unskilled handlers seem to abandon their dogs during visits, ignoring their dogs' communication, focusing more on themselves or people in the environment. This behavior causes stress in dogs and erodes trust to a degree that some dogs learn to anticipate stressful feelings with visiting. All dogs need leaders and visiting dogs are no exception.

Environmental Elements
Together, a dog and a handler create a uniquely balanced team. But they don't visit in a vacuum. They visit in real world settings like schools, nursing homes and hospitals. Within each facility are environmental elements that affect each team's talent and comfort levels, test each team's skill level, and draw from each team's experiences differently.

No matter where teams visit, each environment includes a targeted population, specific goals for that population, a specific number (including none) of staff people involved, a total population, visitors' activity, other activity, other animals, and the physical layout of the facility.

Targeted Population
A person or group being visited is identified differently than the rest of the people in the environment. The targeted populations only include the people for whom the visit is occurring.

Some populations are not appropriate for hands-on animal-enhanced interactions with any dog, no matter how tolerant or talented the dog might be. Sometimes balance requires a different person or population. Staff's role of facilitating each intervention includes screening the targeted population to determine who is appropriate for animal enhanced interactions and who is not.

Specific targeted populations cannot be changed into something they are not, but teams can change which targeted populations they visit. The ways that staff people support and facilitate interventions can be adjusted to lessen the scope of the population's activity. For example, people sitting in chairs are less stimulating to a dog than people walking and wandering about the environment. Visiting active, physically challenging populations with dogs whose talents and comfort levels allow them to enjoy people who behave differently is another way to achieve balance. Visits with individuals tend to be less stressful than visits with groups. Targeted populations with behaviors that are relatively predictable provide less risk than populations whose behaviors cannot be predicted. Increasing staff support helps to balance risks associated with unpredictable populations. Reducing the number of people who are visited at one time helps to balance any environment.

Total Population, Visitors, Other Activity
Most often, only a portion of an entire facility's

population is targeted for each specific intervention. For example, one special education class of ten students might be the targeted population from among three hundred students in one school. The other two hundred and ninety students will make their presence known if given a chance, and so the students and their unsupervised (and so highly unpredictable) behavior must be considered on the environmental side of the balance scale. The effects of maintenance, construction, other social activities, and meal times are among the many other activities that handlers must consider within their visiting environments.

Program Goals and Basic Needs

Staff determine the goals for each targeted population. Skill becomes an important issue when goals are complex and specific. Team skills must be adequate to meet the goals of the program. For example, if walking with a dog is vital to meeting patient mobility goals, an overly exuberant bouncy dog who might pull into the leash or bump into the patient would not be appropriate.

When a population's goals relate mostly to socialization, skill becomes less of an issue than when goals are more complex. Gentle, talented teams who enjoy interactions with unfamiliar people can provide effective opportunities for socialization in quiet, routine settings. Often, the established goal for visiting teams is to create a sense of safety and security. In meeting the basic needs of traumatized people, team skill is not as important as its ability to receive people unconditionally and increase their feelings of safety. It is regrettable when groups dismiss talented teams from visiting effectively in quiet, controlled settings simply because the dog did not demonstrate exemplary obedience skills during an unrelated test. Dogs are sometimes held to arbitrary standards that do not begin to consider individual program goals.

Some groups arbitrarily refuse to accept small dogs into disaster response programs. The benefits provided to traumatized children by Otis and King Tut in the story at the beginning of this chapter illustrate the ways that, indeed, small minimally skilled dogs can be highly effective in meeting goals. The unpredictable targeted population in the story was balanced by the physical layout (the room was large and open), experienced and skilled handlers, and talented dogs. The highly emotional level of the traumatized population was balanced by the number of teams available (three teams) and the high number of volunteer staff people directly involved with the children.

Other Animals

Some handler and dog teams visit alone and sometimes they visit as part of a visiting group with other handlers and dogs. Some facilities have residential animals. A growing number of facilities have begun to allow families to bring pets to visit. Service dogs who accompany people with disabilities have access to clinical and educational settings. Some visiting dogs are unable to maintain focus in the presence of other animals. The best way to make sure interventions remain balanced when dogs don't do well around other animals is for handlers to research facilities with an eye toward other animals prior to making commitments to visit. Dogs who don't do well around other animals require savvy handlers to balance the team.

There is a trend among evaluators to arbitrarily require "dog-to-dog friendliness" (as opposed nice "dog-to-dog manners") among the talents they require every visiting dog to possess, no matter where that dog might visit. Currently some evaluators disqualify dogs from visiting within any program because of sustained eye contact or forward shifts in position toward other dogs, even if the dogs and their handlers demonstrate overall controlled and polite behaviors. Rigid dog-to-dog behavioral standards illustrate the need for more evaluators to understand the concepts that surround balance and compensation. Certainly, facilities that include other animals require careful team selection processes to maintain balance, but teams that include talented dogs who tend to view other dogs with suspicion can still find balance through careful environmental choices and strengthening handler skills. Dogs who are uncontrollably reactive around other dogs probably have other social problems as well; and of course, their behavior would have to improve before they could visit anywhere.

Facility Layout

Facility sites and building designs affect balance. Handlers should make preliminary facility assessments without their dogs. Some of the issues that teams have to deal with include parking, security, bathroom areas for dogs and handlers, floor coverings, cleanliness, and location of targeted population.

Staff Directly Involved

Staff participation carries more weight than any other element on the environmental side of the balance scale. An effective staff can mitigate the risks of visiting with unpredictable populations and enable teams to address complex goals.

Volunteer handlers usually do not have access to much information about the people they visit. A staff person should introduce the person being visited to the team and make the handler aware of any issues that pertain to the visit, such as how best to present the dog (left side of person, right side of person), impairments (such as hearing or visual), frailties, and goals. The care of the person being visited is the direct responsibility of the facility and its staff.

Absence of direct staff participation from any program causes an imbalance that is usually impossible to reconcile. Lack of population control is one of the elements that make "ground zero" disaster response settings so difficult. No one is in charge. The targeted populations are unknown, emotions are raw, and responses are completely unpredictable. Before visiting disaster sites, handlers must carefully consider whether they can remain ethical advocates for their dogs while coping with their own emotions and the behaviors of traumatized people in chaotic surroundings.

Dual-role Handlers

Growing numbers of visiting dogs are actually professional partners with teachers, school counselors, mental health professionals, and therapists. At the end of the workday, they go back home with their handlers and become normal family pet dogs. The popularity of these partnerships is most likely due to the growth of goal-directed animal-enhanced interventions, which are by nature, facilitated by human service professionals. Many human service professionals, who have become aware of the benefits dogs can provide, have determined that the best way to access a consistent canine modality is to have it available continuously. Sometimes, issues that surround confidentiality and scheduling, and the availability of teams who are appropriate to the task preclude participation of volunteer teams. People who work with their own dogs within their professional environments are referred to by this author as dual-role handlers.

Dual-role handlers assume roles and responsibilities on both sides of the balance scale. They are team members on one side and staff on the other. Dual-role handlers present their dogs and facilitate interventions. Human service personnel are, indeed, super people; however, each is only one person. Human service professionals view the people they serve as their primary responsibilities, so they place a primary emphasis on the targeted population (environmental) side of the balance scale.

Most dual-role handlers do not enjoy the luxury of additional staff support as they work with their dogs. Usually, they are the only staff person directly involved with the targeted population. The attention required to fulfill the role of primary staff person leaves less attention available for the team handler position on the other end of the balance scale. Dual-role handlers require dogs who are able to fill any voids left by their multi-tasking teammates. Dogs who work with dual-role handlers must be skilled to the degree that they behave appropriately even in the absence of direct handler attention. It is important that dogs who work with dual-role handlers possess specific skills and talents for the purpose of meeting specific goals. Because dual-role handlers do not enjoy the option of switching environments or changing targeted populations to achieve balance, it is important that they consider the selection and training of their dogs especially carefully.

The Balance Scale

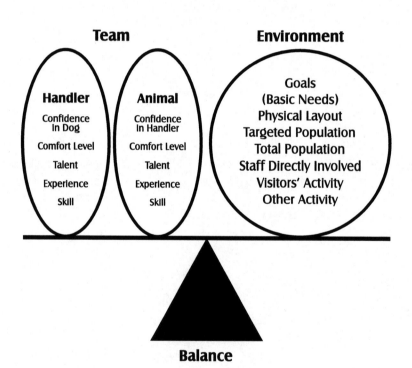

Chapter 9
Trainers and Instructors

I've trained dogs professionally for twenty-five years. More than 1500 dogs have stayed at my boarding school for a minimum of four weeks, and. I've worked with each one. It continues to be an extraordinary opportunity to observe dogs and the people who love them.

Earlier in my career, I trained and handled dogs who earned fifteen American Kennel Club performance titles including Companion Dog (CD) and Companion Dog Excellent (CDX) obedience titles and Junior Hunter (JH) retriever hunting titles. I also coached several people through AKC obedience titles with dogs I had trained for them. One handler was not a client, but my ten-year-old son, Kevin, who earned a CD title with his ten-month-old golden retriever, Partner. I loved the training process and preparing dogs for performance events, but when I left the show ring with my ribbons, I felt less than satisfied with myself. I developed a strong desire to train dogs to really benefit people and I began to direct my education and my marketing efforts toward developing professional relationships with educators and health care providers.

During the same time as I was exploring new options for myself, my son's attention was drifting away from his dog, toward guitars and girls. Lonesome and available, almost by default, Partner became my first professional visiting teammate and seminar assistant. In 1995, Partner and I landed a professional contract to offer therapeutic services at Jim Thorpe Rehabilitation Hospital in Oklahoma City. Finally, I'd found my niche, and it's become increasingly more interesting over time. I feel like the most fortunate trainer in the world every time I exit the clinical and educational "arenas" in which my dogs and I now perform.

Currently my work in rehabilitation includes Meri, a three-year-old Irish Setter, and Whisper, a five-year-old Pomeranian. Both dogs work with therapists to make patients' therapy interesting, functional, and fun. Both dogs are experienced to a degree that, beyond having learned their required skills, they've come to understand their *jobs*. Acquired skills (training) are more crucial to Meri's brand of work than Whisper's. I've developed a number of exercises with Meri that address a wide range of patient goals.

Everyone's favorite seems to be the "duck hunting" exercise. It begins when a patient throws a toy duck, and remembers Meri's retrieving commands. Imagine the patient's sense of control and accomplishment when the dog retrieves, returns, and holds the toy until her patient places a hand beneath the duck and says "Out!" or Meri places the duck in the lap of a patient who cannot use arms or hands. Some patients hunt while standing behind the "duck blind," a sturdy chair with a camouflage-colored flannel sheet over it. Standing exercises encourage patients to practice balance and endurance. Meri is trained to return on cue, jump into the chair, and deliver the duck to her patient. This exercise is followed by praise, petting and mutual admiration. (No training required there.) For Meri's work, her trained, directed delivery to a person other than her handler is a real bonus.

Meri readily assumes a variety of positions. She will stand, lie on the floor, sit up in a chair, or sit or lie on a table. She can be moved, almost effortlessly, in tiny increments to meet the physical needs of the patient with whom she is working.

Satisfaction is a personal thing. For me, it feels more

rewarding every time a patient meets his or her treatment goals while working with one of my dogs than I ever felt from achieving canine performance titles. I'm so grateful for the opportunities to train and work with my dogs in ways that allow me to feel successful. I have made deliberate choices regarding my continuing education, selection of my dogs, my dogs' training, and the shaping of our working environments. Success in any arena seems to relate just as much to the choices people make as it relates to skill.

I feel that handlers who want to visit with their dogs do not have enough options available to them for learning ways to make the best choices for their dogs, for the people they visit, and for themselves. We say, "Handlers need to know..." so many things, but there really are very few places for people to learn the best ways to visit clinical and educational settings with their dogs. I think dog trainers and instructors have long been the missing link. The role of trainers and instructors is to prepare teams to visit.

People who want to develop effective visiting skills with their dogs *require* knowledgeable instructors. The relationship between instructors, visiting dog and handler teams, and the community is reciprocal. The growing popularity of visiting programs offers trainers and instructors new opportunities to create programs that are both personally and professionally satisfying. It's hard to know how many teams are visiting actively. Currently over 15,000 dogs are registered through the three largest national therapy dog organizations in the United States.

Getting started is easy enough for instructors who currently offer solid obedience programs. The first step for any future visiting dog and handler is learning to work dependably as a team in social settings. Most training programs are already structured to accomplish these goals.

Even instructors who lack experience with visiting

programs can teach their clients to be effective handlers. By establishing working relationships with local and national visiting animal organizations, instructors can promote comprehensive programs that transition handlers from training to visiting. Activity within local groups of visiting teams and referrals to those groups from national organizations usually center on the organizations' evaluators/testers. By searching the Internet for both nationally affiliated groups and unaffiliated local groups, instructors should be able to locate all of the evaluators/testers within their region. Instructors can market their courses and gain vital knowledge by volunteering to help with evaluations and observing as many actual visits as possible.

Instructors who coach visiting teams might suggest national registration as a beginning goal for their clients, providing a foundation upon which teams can expand and grow. National therapy dog registration organizations provide liability insurance, but currently only to handlers when they are volunteering, and only when volunteers are visiting within the scope of the organization's specific policies. Instructors should be aware of differing policies, such as permissible equipment, when preparing teams to visit. Instructors should research differing policies carefully to discover which national or local registries work best for their clients. There are choices. Specific information is posted on each organization's Internet site.

Criteria for evaluating tiny visiting dogs differ greatly among registration organizations. Currently, only one national organization's evaluation reflects that tiny dogs usually visit differently than their larger counterparts. The other national organizations use the same process to evaluate a Chihuahua as they use to evaluate a Great Dane. Instructors can direct their handler-clients toward organizations that best meet teams' individual needs.

The current one-test-fits-all approaches to registration have the potential to increase the risk of animal exploitation. Handlers receive blank checks of approval, with only limited understanding of how to evaluate the environment or the dog's responses in the visiting environment. It's not enough to prepare handlers to run through a performance test and send them on their way. Instructors' must prepare their handler-clients for the real world challenges of visiting with their dogs.

Some instructors are also evaluators for national or local organizations. It can be extremely difficult to deal with disgruntled handlers when they do not pass evaluations. Take it from one who's been there; it is even more difficult when the evaluator who did not pass a team is also the instructor who sold the team the training to prepare them for the test they just did not pass! Also, although no impropriety might exist, there is room for the perception of impropriety if the evaluator, whose judgments determine whether a team should visit, has had a previous professional relationship with that team. A more comfortable position is for instructors to teach and coach teams through the process, and allow unrelated sources to provide evaluations and tests in neutral locations.

Weekend events are great for publicity and developing new visiting groups. Instructors who do not have established visiting groups in their communities might consider contracting with a consultant to offer a weekend of training to form a core group of visiting teams.

Blending visiting-specific information into existing basic training programs offers instructors opportunities to attract and effectively prepare people who want to visit with their dogs. This type of program also introduces every client to the possibilities of visiting with their dogs. Nobody loses, and there's potential for tremendous gain.

Therapeutic interactions commonly focus on controlled, enjoyable tactile contact with the dog (touching and petting). This would be the minimal level for handlers to accomplish with their dogs. Animal-enhanced programs have evolved, offering ambitious handlers incentives to continue working with instructors who provide courses that teach handlers how to offer more advanced exercises with their dogs.

Minimal team skills can all be demonstrated on leash. Team skills should be developed to a degree that they can be demonstrated in unfamiliar environments and in the midst of distractions that include unfamiliar people who move and pet dogs in different ways, speak in unusual tones, and use health care equipment.

Handlers must become familiar with ways to reward appropriate behaviors and redirect inappropriate behaviors of their dogs during visits. Although food might be part of ongoing training processes, visiting dogs should be able to receive people without appearing to be focused on pending food rewards. Handlers must become comfortable with techniques for redirecting their dogs without using noticeable corrections during visits. Just as people who handle dogs in competitive sports must learn to transition from training to performing, so beginning handlers must learn to transition from training exercises to presenting their dogs in clinical or educational environments.

Currently the focus on training visiting teams is on the dogs, even though handlers are the team leaders. Handlers are responsible for preparation. Handlers select the environments in which the teams visit. Handlers communicate with staff people and, although the dogs are the stars, handlers also interact with people being visited. Handlers have to know more than their dogs!

Since many volunteer handlers often do not come from human service backgrounds, they must be introduced to issues that surround people who have special needs. In order to adequately prepare handlers, instructors must incorporate lessons that address confidentiality, etiquette, proper terminology regarding people with disabilities, active listening skills, visiting techniques, and issues of infection control and zoonotic concerns.

Most people have never received information about canine signaling and stress symptoms. They think dogs sniff the ground only because the ground smells good. They think their dogs turn away because their dogs are ignoring them. They think their dogs yawn only because they are tired.

However, this trainer's experiences suggest that people accept information about their dogs' communication eagerly and enthusiastically. Seeing behaviors unfold during lessons or seminars has proven to be extremely beneficial in teaching people to rethink their dogs' behavior.

Group lessons provide wonderful opportunities for instructors to show handlers canine communication as it happens. Handlers can observe the difference in some dogs from moment to moment and week to week. Handlers should become aware of instances when their dogs are stressed or aroused to a degree that learning is no longer possible. During lessons, handlers can learn that taking their overwhelmed dogs away from the group or moving to a quieter area, is (indeed!) appropriate handler behavior. Handlers who receive peer approval in class are being prepared to act as their dogs' true advocates during real world visits. Savvy instructors will use canine communication to lead their handler-clients toward discovering for themselves whether or not their dogs are suited to the task of visiting, and which kinds of environments might be best for each dog.

A basic program that includes future visiting teams should introduce walking on leash without pulling, sit, down, coming when called, and a stand. Handlers must practice two "staying" exercises. One "stay" requires that dogs remain at their handlers' sides while exuberant assistants approach, pet the dogs and walk around the teams. It is essential that enthusiastic visiting dogs remain at their handler's side, that they not initiate contact with people in the environment until they receive permission to do so. The other "stay" requires the dog to stay in one position (sit, down, stand) while the handler walks a short distance away and then returns to the dog. It is acceptable for dogs to not take treats from people other than their handlers; however, if they do, dogs must take treats gently. Teams should be able to demonstrate these core behaviors smoothly, with the dog performing capably on either side of the handler, on leash. Currently one national organization's test includes an element that requires dogs to remain calm when left with an unfamiliar person while their handler is out of sight for a few minutes.

Depending on course structure, walking on leash should begin to eventually include handling skills that address walking through and around groups of people and obstacles. Dogs should learn to disregard food and toys on cue. Handlers should begin to purposefully reposition their dogs. Handlers should practice squatting or sitting on floors or in chairs and cuing their dogs from these typical visiting handler positions. Most dogs have to learn to disengage from their handlers when their handlers assume positions other than standing. Instructors and assistants should try different manners of walking and talking while approaching teams, and conduct classes while using health care equipment.

Ready or not, most teams who demonstrate the minimal basic behaviors described so far in this chapter would be able to pass most national visiting animal organizations' evaluation processes. Most handlers want to be the best they can be, and will choose additional training when it is offered. At this point, instructors can offer valuable secondary training, specific to visiting teams.

Visiting team preparation courses offer handlers opportunities to practice positioning skills with their dogs. Different sized dogs require different positioning skills to make them available to the people they are visiting. Small dogs who visit in laps do better on pillows or pads which give them better footing and keep them from falling through between people's legs. Medium-sized dogs seem to be the most awkward to position. They are often too large for laps and too small to be effective on the floor, especially if the people they are visiting are stationed in chairs. Positioning medium-sized dogs in chairs next to seated people is often a very effective technique. Inviting dogs into patients' beds and being positioned in beds should be considered carefully. It is an advanced skill, requiring specific approval and active participation of a staff person for each patient, each visit.

It's important to teach handlers that their dogs are allowed to indicate they are uncomfortable. Handlers can practice adjusting the positioning of their dogs to try to increase the dogs' comfort. Handlers should not force their dogs to remain in any position when the dogs continue to indicate their discomfort.

Instructors must teach their handler-clients that every visit with every person begins with an introduction and ends with a closing, and in between is the time when the dog receives the person being visited. It's a good idea to practice introductions and closings with an instructor or assistants who stand and sit and use health care equipment. Both the dogs and their handlers will be practicing important skills. Visiting team preparation courses should introduce different scenarios that allow handlers to practice responses to situations such as patients who don't want the team to leave, people who think the dogs don't belong in a particular setting, or ways to manage difficult people. Instructors who are not familiar with these issues can recruit nurses, therapists or teachers to help with teaching these concepts. Practice scenarios offer handlers opportunities to experience and master the challenges of eliciting appropriate responses from their dogs while interacting with people who have special needs.

Handlers enrolled in visiting team preparation courses will gain better understanding of infection control if instructors require them to come to class cleaned, groomed, and prepared as though each class were a visit. When instructors require appropriate veterinarian records and discuss conditions that can be passed between people and animals or between animals and people, they teach handlers how to effectively address zoonotic concerns.

It doesn't take long for dogs and their handlers to feel comfortable in the environment in which they train. Once the teams who participate in team preparation courses have developed solid skills, it is appropriate to encourage handlers to find public places in which to practice training between classes.

Local businesses often welcome people who are training their visiting dogs. Usually, only service dogs are allowed in restaurants, but non-food-related establishments can offer teams-in-training wonderful opportunities to enhance their teamwork and basic social skills. Often, all that's needed is to ask.

Some handlers are eager to begin visiting and others will need encouragement and prompting. Instructors who have established working relationships with testers and evaluators from local groups in their communities will be able to refer their clients to upcoming tests and evaluations, making this big step less intimidating. Some training organizations sponsor their own visiting groups made up of their clients. Other instructors encourage their clients to associate with independently established visiting groups and have no connection to the actual visiting process.

Instructors can play an important role in keeping teams fit, even after teams have begun visiting. Some dogs become less attentive to their handlers during visits and some dogs make up new rules as they go along. It can be difficult for handlers to redirect their dogs when they are visiting and, if not addressed, basic skills can deteriorate over time. Instructors can take a proactive stance by developing courses that include teams who are currently visiting. These teams could be included back in basic courses or, if there are numbers to support them, separate refresher courses can be developed. As soon as they begin to consider visiting with their dogs, handler-clients should be made aware that training will be an ongoing process. That way, handlers expect to continue training with their dogs and they appreciate the continuing education opportunities offered by their favorite instructors.

Chapter 10
Heroes Every Day

A small group of people who dubbed themselves "Team Mercy" made a commitment to volunteer with their dogs at The Rehab Center, located within Mercy Hospital in Oklahoma City. For them, "Mercy Thursday" represented the third Thursday evening of every month.

I had worked with two therapists who developed Mercy Hospital's program in 1998. They understood the need for teams who possessed high levels of skills, talent, and experience to meet the program's lofty goals. Each of the teams we identified lived quite a distance from the hospital. In order to be in the hospital's therapy gym by 6:30 p.m., everyone had to travel from outside Oklahoma City through rush hour traffic. Everyone also visited at least one other facility closer to their homes. Still, they all counted Mercy Thursdays as important events, worthy of their effort. Six teams accepted an invitation to participate. Four teams were to be scheduled each time, allowing two teams to be off each month.

Handlers and dogs come in a variety of packages and most people only see the wrapping paper. The dog part of the team package is most apparent. Precious gifts can go unnoticed inside attractive packages. The individual and collective gifts of Team Mercy represent handlers everywhere, not just these six people from Oklahoma, who offer so much more than smiley human faces and hands hanging onto the leashes of their visiting dogs.

Michelle Traw and her yellow Labrador Retriever, Ribs, drove 80 miles round trip. Michelle and Ribs also volunteered at a high school in their city, where they provided goal-directed activities for students with developmental disabilities.

Leslie Sudak and her yellow Labrador Retriever, Cliff, traveled about 70 miles. Leslie, a speech pathologist, also included Cliff in her professional environments. For Leslie, each Mercy Thursday included a full day of work prior to volunteering at the hospital.

Chris and Randy Ann Stickney volunteered as a husband-and-wife team with Bailey, their yellow Labrador Retriever. Both Stickneys worked as school administrators. Bailey often went to work with Chris, and assisted him in dealing with behavioral issues of students with special needs. The Stickneys' drove the furthest, about 140 miles round trip.

Nancy Keiser and her Vizsla, Mariah, drove almost 50 miles round trip. Nancy also donated considerable time to coordinate scheduling of the teams for this program. Nancy and Mariah also visited a dialysis center regularly and presented responsible pet ownership programs to schoolchildren.

Sherry Gibson and her Golden Retriever, Sunny, drove about 65 miles round trip. Sherry and Sunny volunteered in a special education program for elementary school children and also promoted animal-enhanced programs in their community.

My seventeen-year-old daughter, Manda, and her Pomeranian, King Tut, were also a part of this group. Because of the complicated 85-mile round-trip drive, my husband and I drove Manda and her dog to the hospital and then waited for them in a small adjoining room. Manda and King Tut also volunteered during summer breaks at a hospital for children with developmental disabilities.

To everyone but the handlers, Mercy Thursdays appeared to begin when the teams walked into the gym, where about fifteen patients usually sat in wheelchairs, waiting. After briefly introducing themselves, each team reported to their "station." Each station was staffed by a physical, occupational, or speech therapist and the patients were rotated in small groups among the stations. After about an hour, when the patients had met their goals at each station, the teams were finished for the night. A therapist accompanied them back out through the hospital and they made their long trips home.

Most people don't realize the depth of handler commitment that surrounds every visiting dog. Handlers' gifts are the details that usually go unseen. There are thousands of volunteer teams visiting all across the United States whose handlers bathe and groom their dogs and shuffle hectic family schedules to take a walk with a patient, or listen to a child read, or offer a scared or lonely person a few minutes of unconditional support.

American culture seems to value image, prosperity, achievement, and approval above all else. Success is defined, measured, and esteemed in degrees of "how much" and "compared to what" in every aspect of life. It's easy for people today to lose sight of their own self-worth in their search for approval from others.

Ironically, discussion of human values provides insight into the connection most people feel with appropriate dogs. Dogs are exactly the opposite! People safely assume that no dog is concerned with their human's appearance, nor do dogs make judgments based on any human's financial or personal status. Dogs don't care about clothes or correct grammar. Dogs live in the moment. Past achievements, mistakes, and physical changes that have occurred in the lives of people they are visiting seem irrelevant to dogs. People being received by visiting dogs do not have to earn approval; approval and acceptance are freely given.

How differently some handlers judge themselves and their own worth! Media attention surrounding the events in New York City following September 11 resulted in a new public perception of visiting dogs as heroes. Images of dogs comforting victims and workers at the World Trade Center have been used to promote everything from national disaster relief organizations to local breed clubs and, particularly, to promote visiting animal organizations. In response to increased interest and perceptions of more "worthy" achievements, visiting organizations have developed definitions and tests (measures) that set one team apart from others, labeling teams as being more – and less – "approved."

No one should accept the premise that working with traumatized people is for a select few. There are more opportunities to respond than most people imagine. Within each community, there are important roles and responsibilities for every visiting team. Trauma and loss are personal events. Most personal catastrophes do not attract media attention. Unless visiting in the media spotlight is a goal, handlers can commit to programs which provide comfort and teach coping skills to traumatized people on a regular basis within their own communities.

Based on figures from the year 2000, more than two million people are injured in car accidents in the United States each year, many severely. These traumatized patients and their families often grieve the loss of life as they knew it, as well as the loss of some ability. Teams who regularly visit patients in community critical care and rehabilitation hospitals are presented with opportunities to interact with victims of motor vehicle accidents, gun shots, fires, industrial accidents, and other traumatic events that can happen in any community.

Some teams visit in community settings that prevent disaster. No one will ever see media coverage on a child's prevented suicide. Among young people fifteen to twenty-four years of age, suicide is the third-leading cause of death in the United States. In 2003, sixty-six Oklahoma youth killed themselves. My state ranks twenty-seventh in population in the nation, but ninth in the nation for youth suicides. Those statistics both disturb me and move me into action. Likewise, visiting teams across the country offer educators, therapists and counselors creative ways to work with young people who are at-risk in schools, youth shelters, sexual abuse treatment centers, and drug and alcohol treatment programs.

It is traumatic for elementary school students who have fallen behind in reading to practice their skills in groups made up of human peers. "They laugh at me," is a common response. Their apprehensions toward reading can cause these children to fall hopelessly behind. Young children who don't learn to read grow into students who are unable to learn. People who cannot read are absolutely at risk in our society. Volunteer programs that include visiting dogs and their handlers as reading coaches for children are springing up in community schools throughout the United States. Children whose confidence has been destroyed feel comfortable reading to attentive dogs. Ordinary people are making an extraordinary difference by taking dogs into schools and listening.

Throughout the United States, handlers make time in hectic schedules to bathe and groom dogs and drive to community settings in which they visit. Handlers do the preparatory work, knowing their dogs will get the credit. Teachers, counselors, therapists, and activities directors sometimes work with their own dogs; but more often they depend on some of the thousands of dependable volunteers who show up weekly or monthly to offer their special brand of healing and education. It's impossible to measure one team's worth against another's. Handlers who feel pressure from peers to be "more" need only to look deep into their dogs' eyes to appreciate the every-day hero in the reflection. Handlers can benefit from receiving the same message their dogs deliver every time they visit: "You are just right. We are just right. This is enough."

My craft combines dogs with health care and education in ways that encourage people to meet functional goals. I am certain that I was born at just the right time. Dogs have always been here; but we humans are just now discovering ways to tap into their phenomenal gifts. We've begun that process, and now it's time to discover whether what we ask of them measures up to what each individual dog is designed to give. Humans have a history of using natural resources indiscriminately, then feeling sorry afterward. Our obligation now is to serve as our dogs' advocates, appreciating them for just who and what they are, and *not* projecting our images of success onto them. That's exactly what our dogs do for us. Their best gifts are the looks that say, "I love you, man. You're just right." Our obligation is to return the gift.

Resources

Seminars and Services
Reaching People Through Dogs Programs
Kris Butler
405-364-7650
www.DogPrograms.com

National Visiting Animal Registries
Therapy Dogs Incorporated
877-843-7364
www.therapydogs.com

Delta Society Pet Partners
425-226-7357
www.deltasociety.org

Therapy Dogs International, Inc.
973-252-9800
www.tdi-dog.org

Service Dogs, Assistance Dogs
International Association of Assistance Dog Partners
586-826-3938
www.iaadp.org

References

Beck, Alan and Aaron Katcher. Between Pets and People. West Lafayette, Indiana: Purdue University Press. 1996.

Butrick, Ann. "Changing Tears into Smiles in the Beginning." No posting date. Therapy Dogs Inc. 9 Feb. 2004 <http://www.therapydogs.com/inbeginning.htm>.

Coppinger, Lorna and Raymond Coppinger. Dogs. New York: Scribner. 2001.

De Becker, Gavin. Fear Less. Boston: Little, Brown and Company. 2002.

De Becker, Gavin. The Gift of Fear. Boston: Little, Brown and Company. 1997.

Deeley, Martin. "How It All Began." No posting date. International Association of Canine Professionals. 9 Feb. 2004 <http://www.dogpro.org/articles/howitbegan.htm>.

Fast, Julius. Body Language. New York: Simon and Schuster Pocket Books. 1971.

Froling, Joan. "Language Confusion." Partners Forum. Sept. 2002. p. 12.

Rugaas, Turid. On Talking Terms with Dogs: Calming Signals. Carlsborg, WA: Legacy by Mail. 1997.

"Application and Interview Pitfalls." No posting date. Personnel Policy Services. 12 Feb. 2004 <http://www.ppspublishers.com/articles/resources/#OSHA>.

"A Brief History." No posting date. Therapy Dogs International, Inc. 9 Feb. 2004 <http://www.tdi-dog.org/briefhistory.html>.

"Performance Evaluations." No posting date. Personnel Policy Services. 12 Feb. 2004 <http://www.ppspublishers.com/articles/resources/#OSHA>.

"Pet Partners Program." 6 Feb. 2004. Delta Society. 9 Feb. 2004. <http://www.deltasociety.org/dsa000.htm>.

"Risky Business: A Primer on Reference Checking." No posting date. Personnel Policy Services. 12 Feb. 2004 <http://www.ppspublishers.com/articles/resources/#OSHA>.

Also from Kris Butler and Funpuddle Publishing Associates

Therapy Dogs: Compassionate Modalities
Roles and Goals for Clinical Environments

This 46-minute DVD includes 7 vignettes that will take viewers from warm and fuzzy visits into goal directed interventions, with over 80 functional patient goals identified. Additionally, the skills of both large and small dogs are identified throughout.

The book points out and discusses important issues relating to the roles and behaviors of handler, dogs, and staff, as well as repeating information from the DVD.

Individual copies of this book/DVD are available at www.DogPrograms.com and through the usual Internet book sites. With approval, books without DVDs are available from the publisher for group presentations of the DVD.

Groups and instructors may contact Funpuddle Publishing Associates at 405-364-7650 or Seminars@DogPrograms.com for generous discounts on quantity purchases of *Therapy Dogs Today: Their Gifts, Our Obligation* and *Therapy Dogs: Compassionate Modalities*.

eaching People Through Dogs Programs

Seminars and services are delivered throughout the United States by Kris Butler. For information about hosting an event, email Seminars@DogPrograms.com or phone (405)364-7650.

Seminars

- Building Blocks
- Therapeutic by Design
- Professional Designs for Educators
- Professional Designs for Health Care Professionals
- Professional Designs for Dog Trainers
- What about THIS Dog? (How to Assess)

Services

- Environmental Assessment
- Dog and Handler Assessment
- Mentoring and Coaching

About the Author

Kris Butler is a nationally recognized trainer, instructor and authority on animal-enhanced programs. She's developed goal directed programs for therapists and special education teachers from throughout the United States, and she has worked professionally with her own dogs in therapeutic environments since 1995. She has provided professional consulting, evaluator training, site assessment, and animal evaluation services for Delta Society in Hawaii, Wyoming, Texas, Boston, New York, Washington, Ohio, Arkansas, and Oklahoma. Hundreds of handlers and program administrators have attended her Reaching People Through Dogs seminars. For more than ten years, she evaluated volunteer teams for Delta Society and Therapy Dogs, Inc. She is an adjunct faculty member in University of Denver's Graduate School of Social Work, contributing to development and instruction of the online Animals and Human Health certificate program. Since 1979, her professional vision has focused on working with dogs to improve the quality of peoples' lives.

It's been said that animals open doors so that healing can begin. Let us humans always listen so that we hear opportunities knocking on those doors, and creatively work with our dogs to walk through – then discover the endless possibilities inside.

A quote from the author, as she accepted Delta Society's 1995 Therapy Dog of the Year Award with Partner